THE "WE KNOWS" OF THE APOSTLE PAUL

HOLMES ROLSTON

# THE "WE KNOWS" OF THE
# apostle paul

JOHN KNOX PRESS
Richmond, Virginia

LIBRARY OF CONGRESS CATALOG CARD NUMBER: 66-12114
© M. E. BRATCHER 1966
PRINTED IN THE UNITED STATES OF AMERICA
J.3200

*Dedicated to the congregation of the Trinity Presbyterian Church of Richmond, Virginia. It was in the setting of proclamation and response as experienced in the pulpit of this church that these sermons were called into being.*

# PREFACE

Is it possible for a man today to come to an assured knowledge of the answers to the great ultimate questions that deal with the meaning of his human existence? Can he know with certainty that there is a God? Can he be confident that this God has made himself known to man? Can he know with certainty that the God of the universe is a personal Being who knows and loves him? Can he lay hold of a moral absolute in the midst of the vast secularism of the modern world? Can he face death in the confidence that for him there is a life beyond the grave?

This book seeks to answer these and similar questions. It does this by taking its stand with the Apostle Paul as he identifies himself with the believing community of the New Testament. It listens to him as he speaks for himself and for the church of which he is a part in a series of great affirmations which begin with the words "we know." It discovers in them the faith of the church of the New Testament as this believing community points beyond itself to the living Lord.

The first two chapters set forth an epistemology, a theory of knowledge, the theory of knowledge that is at the heart of the testimony of the first Christians. These believing men and women of the New Testament know that men enter into an assured knowledge of the things of God only as they respond in repentance, faith, love, and obedience to the proclamation of that which God has done for man in Jesus Christ. They know that to those who have made the response of faith there does come a knowledge of the wisdom of God, an understanding of the mind of Christ, which is foolishness or offense to the wisdom of the world.

The chapters which follow set forth the knowledge which was

at the heart of the faith and life of the New Testament church. They begin, where New Testament proclamation begins, with the witness to the resurrection of Jesus Christ from the dead. They are written in the awareness of the limitations of our human knowledge in the days of our flesh but also in the certainty that God through Christ has given to those who will receive them the insights of faith that give meaning to their human existence.

The sermons in this book set forth the "we knows" of the Apostle Paul. Most of them are based on texts which begin with the words "we know." Others are developed from texts that carry a similar idea in different language. They seek to examine the "we knows" of the Apostle Paul as affirmations of faith that are inevitable when men have heard the word that was spoken through Jesus Christ. These affirmations are seen both in their setting in the Pauline Epistles and in their relevance for life today.

As we examine the content of that body of truth which is set forth in the "we knows" of Paul, we come to the realization that we have here a creed that is common to the various branches of the Christian church today. The affirmations which are proclaimed in the "we knows" of Paul could become the themes of sermons to be preached to Protestants, to Roman Catholics, or to those who stand in the Greek Orthodox tradition. In the "we knows" of Paul we have a statement of the faith of the church in the beginning. We have at the same time an element of ecumenical encounter. The faith which is proclaimed here is the faith of every church that finds in the New Testament the source of its message. We should not underestimate the abiding importance of the things upon which Christians today cannot agree. But it is significant that in the "we knows" of Paul we have a statement of faith in which Christians can unite as they face the secularism, the humanism, and the atheism of the modern world.

In his "we knows," Paul takes his stand with the believing community of the New Testament and interprets the faith of this community. He speaks from the community and to the community and through the community to all who have ears to hear. He speaks as the apostle of Jesus Christ who must communicate the message given to him as the Word of the Lord for all mankind.

# CONTENTS

# I

## THE WISDOM OF GOD

*Scripture Background—1 Corinthians 1:17-25.*

"For Jews demand signs and Greeks seek wisdom, but we preach Christ crucified, a stumbling block to Jews and folly to Gentiles, but to those who are called, both Jews and Greeks, Christ the power of God and the wisdom of God."—1 Corinthians 1:22-24.

Is there a knowledge of God at the heart of the Christian community that is not to be found at any other place? In this text, Paul insists that to the called—that is, to the *ecclesia*, the church—there has been entrusted a wisdom of God which was not known in the secular world. He takes his stand with the church of the New Testament as he says, "We know the wisdom of God and the power of God." The first Christians found in the proclamation of Christ crucified the key to the understanding of life's mysteries and the source of a redemptive power that was available to them in their time of need.

As Paul went up and down the Graeco-Roman world telling the story of Jesus Christ and him crucified, he found that to many of the Jews his message was a word of offense, a stumbling block. He found also that many of the Gentiles considered his message to be the height of folly. But he knew that through the proclamation of the gospel there was coming into being a small body of believers. Some of these believers were Jews and others were Gentiles, but to the members of this church, regardless of their background, Christ Jesus was the wisdom of God, the answer of God to life's deepest questions, and the power of God, the source of power for victorious living. The question the text raises is: How is it that the preaching of Christ crucified can be to some offense and folly and to others wisdom and power?

As Paul looks out on his world, he describes the Jews as he says, "Jews demand signs." The Jews were waiting for the coming of the Messiah. They were expecting an "Anointed of the Lord" to lead them into their destiny. But before they would commit themselves they demanded signs. We hear this demand for a sign in connection with the crucifixion of the Christ. Matthew tells us that those who passed by Jesus while he was on the cross derided him, saying, "You who would destroy the temple and build it in three days, save yourself! If you are the Son of God, come down from the cross." In the same setting, the scribes and elders mocked him, saying, "He saved others; he cannot save himself. He is the King of Israel; let him come down now from the cross, and we will believe in him" (Matthew 27:41-42). Jesus described this kind of demand for signs as an expression of the spirit of an evil and adulterous generation (Matthew 12:39). His coming was not without signs. The movement of the Gospel of John is centered around a series of signs. But these were signs to call forth faith. They were in part veiled. John can sum up his picture of the unbelief of Israel as he says of the leaders of the Jews: "Though he had done so many signs before them, yet they did not believe in him" (John 12:37). What the Jews who rejected Jesus wanted was not a sign leading to faith but a sign that would render the venture of faith unnecessary. They wanted to walk by sight, not by faith. The leaders of the Jews are not alone in this demand. In every age there are those who wish to escape from the indirect communication of the gospel to find a way of life that does not require the venture of faith.

Paul describes the Greeks as he says, "Greeks seek wisdom." The Greeks were not looking for signs. They had no expectance of a divine intervention in human history. They were seeking wisdom. The Greeks sought to come to an understanding of themselves and their universe. We must pay a high tribute to the Greeks in their search for wisdom. They had produced philosophers such as Socrates, Plato, and Aristotle. These men will always remain among the great in the world of philosophy. Their civilization had flowered in literature, sculpture, and art. They had produced great statesmen such as Pericles. The debt of mankind to what the Greeks had produced in their search for wisdom cannot be overestimated. But the Greeks had not found the answer to the ultimate questions of human existence. When Paul stood in Athens, the center of Greek culture, his spirit was moved within him because he saw the city wholly given to idolatry.

Far more important to us than the quest for wisdom which we find in the Greeks and the Romans is the quest for wisdom which we find in science today. Men have sought by the various disciplines of the sciences to enter into an understanding of the structure of their universe. The modern world in many of its most significant aspects has been created by the capacity of man to grow in his understanding of the secrets of his universe and by his ability to use his knowledge for his own purposes. The marvel of the modern world is man's increasing mastery of his universe. No one would question the importance of man's effort to increase his knowledge of the world in which he lives. In terms of the conveniences of civilization no one would wish to move back to the primitive living of the world of Paul. But we would have some questions as to the wisdom of a secularism which assumes that man by his own efforts can discover all he needs to know about the world in which he lives.

Into the world of Corinth where the Jews were demanding signs and the Greeks were seeking wisdom, Paul went as one whom Christ had sent to preach the gospel. He writes to the Corinthians: "I decided to know nothing among you except Jesus Christ and him crucified" (1 Corinthians 2:2). In our text he says, "We preach Christ crucified." His statements sound very simple, but they have far-reaching implications. When Paul made his start in Thessalonica, he began by proving to the Jews from their Scriptures that it was necessary for the Christ to suffer and die and to rise from the dead. After he had laid this foundation, he said to them: "This Jesus, whom I proclaim to you, is the Christ" (Acts 17:3). Paul insisted that it was necessary for the Christ to suffer and die. He followed Jesus himself in fusing the concept of the Messiah with the prophetic picture of the suffering servant. We can be sure that Paul told in Corinth the story of the life and death of Jesus. We can be sure also that he gave his witness to the resurrection. You cannot give the witness to the resurrection without first telling the story of the death of the Christ. But you cannot preach Christ crucified without moving on to testify to the resurrection. You cannot call men to living faith in a dead Christ. The Christ of the Scriptures is the one who can say of himself: "Fear not, I am the first and the last, and the living one; I died, and behold I am alive for evermore, and I have the keys of Death and Hades" (Revelation 1:17-18). Paul writes to the Corinthians: "I delivered to you as of first importance what I also received, that Christ died for our sins in accordance with the scriptures, that he was buried, that he was raised on the third day in accordance with the scriptures" (1 Corinthians 15:3-4). Paul gave in Corinth the testimony to the crucified and risen Lord.

Paul says that to many of the Jews this testimony to a suffering and dying Messiah was a stumbling block. The Jews were looking for a world-conquering Messiah who would come as a son of David, an Anointed of the Lord to deliver them from their enemies and to set up at Jerusalem a kingdom in which the Jews would be the conquering people. They could not fit the facts of the life of Jesus into their concept of the Messiah. And they were not interested in his call to them to become the people of the suffering servant. Jesus still confronts us as a man of offense. His call to us is the call to renounce ourselves, to take up our cross daily and follow him. He promises us great satisfactions, but these promises are not to be realized unless first we know the meaning of renunciation and suffering service. He shows us a way of life, but he says that we must lose our life for his sake if we are to find it. In the nature of his call to men he is still the man of offense.

Paul says that to many of the Gentiles his preaching of Christ crucified was a word of folly. The Greeks and the Romans were committed to the quest for wisdom, but they could not believe that the clue to the meaning of their human existence was to be found in the story of a crucified Jew and in the witness of a few men to his resurrection. If Paul's testimony was difficult for the Greeks and the Romans to accept, it is equally difficult for modern man to receive. We can pause here to express our full appreciation of the quest for wisdom as it is found in science today. Our protest would

be to those apostles of science who brand as "folly" every other
effort to come by a different road to an understanding of the meaning of our human existence. Is it not possible for the man of science
to wonder if the God who has put us here has taken the initiative
and come to us in the context of our history? We do not question
the way of science. We can question arrogance in the use of the
way of science.

Paul's preaching of Christ crucified was to the Jews a stumbling
block and to the Greeks folly. But Paul knew that he had seen the
coming into being of a group which he names "the called." He says
in verse 18: "The word of the cross is folly to those who are perish-
ing, but to us who are being saved it is the power of God." The
church was the community of those who had believed Paul's message. In one sense it was the community of those whom God had
called out of the secular world to become his church. In another
sense it was the community of those who had responded in faith
and obedience to the proclamation of the gospel. In the mystery of
proclamation and response, the church had come into being.

To this community, Christ was the wisdom of God. If you had
asked the people of this community concerning God they would
have said that they had seen the light of the knowledge of the glory
of God in the face of Jesus Christ (2 Corinthians 4:6). They knew
the love of God which was in Jesus Christ their Lord. They knew
the power of God in his bringing from the dead the Lord Jesus
Christ through the blood of the everlasting covenant. They had
found in Paul's preaching of Christ crucified the answer to their
questions concerning God and man and human destiny. This
knowledge of God which was to be found at the heart of this community was not the product of wishful thinking. It had come to
them because they had heard that which God was saying to man
in Jesus Christ. The great affirmations that came from the heart of
this believing community were not true just because these people
believed them. They were true because this was the way in which
God had disclosed himself to man.

Deeper than the question of wisdom is the question of power.
These Christians had found the secret of victorious living. In their
knowledge of their acceptance as children of God and in their

response in love to that which God had done for them in Jesus Christ, the Christians in Corinth had found power for righteous living. They had found also the hope of an eternal redemption through which in time they would be delivered from this present evil world to find their place in the eternal kingdom of God.

How is it that the word of the cross is wisdom and power to some and offense and folly to others? The answer is to be found in the element of personal response. God has come to us in Jesus Christ and we are responsible for the way in which we respond to him. The great affirmations of the Christian faith are true quite independently of whether or not we believe them. But they have redemptive power in our lives only as we believe the good news of the proclamation of Christ crucified.

The great affirmations of the Christian faith cannot be laid hold of by the detached spectator. If we are to enter into them we must begin with the response of faith in which we acknowledge Jesus as Savior and Lord. If we are to enter into the fullness of their understanding we must enter upon the pilgrimage of faith. In such a pilgrimage it is possible to come to assured knowledge in which we go beyond the wisdom of man to a knowledge of the things that are to be found only in the wisdom of God.

# II

## THE MIND OF CHRIST

*Scripture Background—1 Corinthians 2:1-16.*

"We have the mind of Christ."—1 Corinthians 2:16.

It is a bold and almost arrogant statement for Paul to insist that those who stand at the heart of the Christian community have the mind of Christ. We need therefore to look closely at the setting in which he makes this statement. In the second chapter of First Corinthians, Paul is discussing the work of the Holy Spirit in enabling a man to believe the gospel and in opening up to the believer the full significance of that which God has done for man in Jesus Christ. In the first chapter he has dealt with the way in which the preaching of Christ crucified has become to the Jews a stumbling block and to the Greeks foolishness, but to the called, both Jews and Greeks, the power of God and the wisdom of God. He has suggested that there is at the heart of the believing community, the church, a body of knowledge concerning God and his will for man that is not to be found at any other place. In the second chapter, he is still concerned with the contrast between the wisdom of man and the wisdom of God which has been entrusted to the church. Paul believes that the knowledge of God that is to be found in the Christian community has come as the Holy Spirit has brought home to those who have heard the proclamation of the gospel the truth of its message. He says that no man knows the mind of a man except the spirit of the man which is in him. In a similar way he insists that the Spirit of Christ knows the mind of Christ and that he has led the Christian community to something of an understanding of the mind of the Christ. The Christian community which has in some measure the mind of the Christ possesses a wisdom of God which stands in sharp contrast to the wisdom of the secular world.

Paul says that the Christians have a wisdom. It is not a wisdom of the secular world. The rulers of this world did not have this wisdom when they faced Jesus of Nazareth. If they had had this wisdom, they would not have crucified the Lord of glory. The rulers of this world did crucify the Lord of glory. Paul writes to the Galatians: "When the time had fully come, God sent forth his Son, born of woman" (Galatians 4:4). But the rulers of this world did not recognize the Son of God as he moved in the context of their world.

Concerning the wisdom of man, Paul makes two statements. The first is that the world through wisdom did not know God. The second is that it is the wisdom of God that man in his own wisdom should not find God (1 Corinthians 1:21). Consider, for example, the wisdom of the Greeks. In their quest for wisdom, the Greeks came to know many things, but they did not come to a knowledge of God. This statement is equally true of modern man. In the wisdom of science man has come to know many things about the structure of his universe. He can use this knowledge as he seeks to enter into his earth and subdue it. But the knowledge of God is not to be found through the telescope or the microscope. Modern man when he refuses to listen to the wisdom of God is as ignorant of the answers to the ultimate questions of his existence as was the man of the ancient world.

But Paul is confident that those who stand within the community of the called, the community of those who have heard what God is saying to man in Jesus Christ, do possess a wisdom of God. He describes this as a secret and hidden wisdom. This wisdom is hidden in the sense that man could not discover it. It is secret in the sense that it was a mystery which had to be disclosed. It is not secret in the sense that those who know it are trying to keep the secret among themselves. Instead they are trying in every way they can to disclose it to the world. But the world cannot hear it because the world will not meet the conditions for receiving it.

This mystery includes some knowledge of the things which God has prepared for those who love him. In verse 9 Paul describes this wisdom of God. He says there has been revealed to us

"What no eye has seen, nor ear heard,
nor the heart of man conceived,
what God has prepared for those who love him."

The language of this verse has often been used to describe the
things that Christians will discover after they enter through death
into the resurrection world of God. It is unquestionably true that
there is much that will be known then that is not known now. But
Paul is not talking about the things we will learn when we know
as we are known. He is talking about the things that Christians
know now. This is shown by the tenth verse, in which Paul tells
us that these are the things which "God has revealed to us through
the Spirit." The Christian already knows what, apart from revelation, no eye has seen, nor ear heard, nor the heart of man conceived.
The Christian is not without some knowledge of the things which
God has prepared for those who love him.

How can this knowledge which is at the heart of the Christian
community be communicated? As we seek to answer this question
we must remember that Paul lived in a world which was filled with
the so-called mystery religions. Those who founded these religions
claimed to possess a secret understanding of life which they would
communicate only to those who joined them. We have some parallel
to this in secret orders which exist today and disclose their care-
fully guarded secrets only to the initiated. With much of this kind
of thing Paul would have had absolutely no patience. Christianity
is not a mystery religion which discloses its secrets only to the
initiated. The great affirmations of the Christian faith are made
boldly in the marketplace. They are made for all to hear.

But there is an inescapable condition for the receiving of the
wisdom of God. The proclamation of Christ crucified is heard when
the Holy Spirit witnesses to its truth in the heart of the one who
hears the proclamation. Paul, Timothy, and Silas went to Thessalonica. They told there as they told in Corinth the story of the
life, death, and resurrection of Jesus Christ. There were many who
did not receive the message, but there were others who did. There
was called into being in Thessalonica a community of those who received the message of Paul for what it was; that is, as the word

of God. In describing his experience in Thessalonica Paul writes:
"We know, brethren beloved by God, that he has chosen you; for
our gospel came to you not only in word, but also in power and in
the Holy Spirit and with full conviction" (1 Thessalonians 1:4).
The Thessalonians were convinced of the truth of the gospel because they had received in their hearts the witness of the Holy
Spirit.

In similar vein Paul writes to the Corinthians, telling them that
no man will ever be moved by the Spirit to say, "Jesus be cursed!"
This was the phrase which their persecutors asked the Christians
to repeat as the repudiation of their faith. Paul is certain that the
Spirit will never lead a man to deny his faith. And then he adds:
"and no one can say 'Jesus is Lord' except by the Holy Spirit"
(1 Corinthians 12:3).

Paul is affirming here the same thing that Jesus himself taught
when he said to Nicodemus: "Truly, truly, I say to you, unless
one is born anew, he cannot see the kingdom of God." Jesus continues: "Truly, truly, I say to you, unless one is born of water and
the Spirit, he cannot enter the kingdom of God" (John 3:3, 5). The
condition of becoming a part of the Christian community is to believe in the heart the good news of the gospel and to make public
profession of this faith before men. John tells us the same thing
when in the prologue to his Gospel he writes of the Christ: "He
came to his own home, and his own people received him not. But
to all who received him, who believed in his name, he gave power
to become children of God; who were born, not of blood nor of the
will of the flesh nor of the will of man, but of God" (John 1:11-13).

The faith that enables us to enter into an understanding of the
wisdom of God comes through the testimony of the Holy Spirit in
the heart. The realization of this fact need not lead us to despair.
God is ready to give the Spirit to those who will receive him. Jesus
says: "What father among you, if his son asks for a fish, will instead of a fish give him a serpent; or if he asks for an egg, will
give him a scorpion? If you then, who are evil, know how to give
good gifts to your children, how much more will the heavenly
Father give the Holy Spirit to those who ask him!" (Luke 11:11-
13). God will give the Holy Spirit to those who will receive him.

If we do not harden our hearts and resist the Spirit he will bring home to us the truth of the gospel message.

But the communication of the wisdom of God is not completed when men make the initial act of surrender and are ready to receive it. In the life of the Christian community there is a continuing process of seeking to lead the members of this community to an ever deepening understanding of the meaning of their faith and of its significance for all of life. Paul writes to the Corinthians: "Yet among the mature we do impart wisdom" (1 Corinthians 2:6). The mature are those who have passed beyond the first principles to the readiness to enter into an understanding of the deeper things of the Christian life. Paul writes to the Colossians of the way in which God has chosen to make known to his saints the "mystery, which is Christ in you, the hope of glory." He continues: "Him we proclaim, warning every man and teaching every man in all wisdom, that we may present every man mature in Christ" (Colossians 1:27-28). He writes to the Corinthians: "We have received . . . the Spirit which is from God, that we might understand the gifts bestowed on us by God. And we impart this in words not taught by human wisdom but taught by the Spirit, interpreting spiritual truths to those who possess the Spirit" (1 Corinthians 2:12-13). Paul himself has taken his stand with the Christian community and has sought with the leaders of this community to understand what God has done for man in Jesus Christ. He has entered into the knowledge of the things of God as the Spirit has disclosed them to him. In this sense he possesses the wisdom of God; or, to use his daring phrase, he has the mind of Christ. He seeks to communicate this knowledge to those who are able to understand it. It is here that we come to what might be called the "we knows" of Paul. They are the times when Paul takes his stand within the framework of the Christian faith and gives expression to the things that are known in the community of faith. Often his expressions are almost incidental as he is discussing some other problem. But they are not expressions of Paul's personal prejudices. They are the affirmation of convictions that should be common to all those who have entered into the inner meaning of the Christian faith. A typical example of this is in 1 Corinthians 8:4, when he is discussing the question of eating meat offered to idols and throws in almost as an aside: "We know that 'an idol has no real existence,' and that 'there is no God but one.' "

In these statements Paul is not dealing with truths that have no objective reality. He is not just stating the convictions of Christians. He is saying that Christians believe these things because they are part of the disclosure of himself which God has made in Christ. He is not dealing with illusions but with affirmations of the knowledge which God has entrusted to men.

But Paul knows that the truths he is proclaiming cannot be laid hold of by the detached spectator who is unwilling to become personally involved in the revelation of himself which God has given in Christ. It is in this setting that he writes: "The unspiritual man does not receive the gifts of the Spirit of God, for they are folly to him, and he is not able to understand them because they are spiritually discerned" (1 Corinthians 2:14). We have here a theory of knowledge in which the effective apprehension of the wisdom of God is limited to those who respond in faith, love, and obedience to God's disclosure of himself in Jesus Christ.

We should not disparage the wisdom of man. The efforts of man to understand the laws of his universe have taught us much concerning its structure. But the ultimate answers to the questions of humanity are not, and never have been, in the flesh. There is at the heart of the Christian church a wisdom of God. Paul speaks for the Christian community when he says, "We have the mind of Christ." In the "we knows" of Paul we have some insights into the mind of the Christ and some knowledge of the wisdom of God.

It is through the wisdom of God that we come to the assured knowledge that Jesus is indeed the Christ, the Son of God, and to the confidence that we can entrust to him the salvation of our souls. It is here that we come to know that this present life is a time of testing and preparation for the life that lies beyond death. It is in the wisdom of God that we learn to see all men as potentially children of God with the possibility of an eternal destiny. It is here that we receive the insights that enable us to find abiding significance in our human existence.

# III

# THE WITNESS TO THE RESURRECTION

*Scripture Background—1 Corinthians 15:1-19.*

"We testified of God that he raised Christ."—1 Corinthians 15:15.

The testimony to the resurrection of Jesus Christ from the dead was central to the preaching of Paul and the apostles. It is a fact of history that after the crucifixion of Jesus of Nazareth by Pontius Pilate there emerged a group of people who said that after his suffering and death Jesus Christ had presented himself alive to them, that he had appeared to them over a period of forty days, and that he had spoken to them of the kingdom of God (Acts 1:3). The knowledge of the resurrection of Jesus was at the heart of the New Testament testimony to him. It was from this center that the first preachers of Christianity moved out in their proclamation of the message which had been committed to them. They saw the life of Jesus and the death of Jesus in the light of his resurrection. They moved from their knowledge of Christ's resurrection to their certainty of his victory over sin and death and to their certainty of the existence of a resurrection world of God that lies beyond death. The belief in the resurrection of Jesus Christ was an article of faith which Paul had received from those who were Christians before him. He had proclaimed this part of the creed of the Christians to the Corinthians and had set forth to them the supporting evidence. They had believed his message. Paul and the other apostles and the Corinthians were in complete agreement in their acceptance of the truth of the testimony to the resurrection.

What was it that these Christians actually believed concerning the resurrection of Jesus Christ? They knew that Jesus was dead, that he was pronounced dead by the centurion whom Pilate had sent to investigate, and that his dead body was buried in the tomb of Joseph of Arimathea. They knew that on the morning of the third day the tomb was found empty. Their belief in the resurrection went beyond the belief that the spirit of Jesus survived the separation of the soul and body at death. They believed that after three days, life came back into the dead body.

Their belief went beyond what we might call resusitation. Life came back into the body of Lazarus. But Lazarus emerged from the tomb with a body similar to that which we have now. He still had to face death. In contrast, Jesus experienced a resurrection body that was in many ways different from the body the disciples had known. There was continuity but there was also transformation. Because they believed that he was alive, the early Christians believed that Jesus could be spiritually present with his people.

What are the foundations of the faith of the first Christians in the resurrection of their Lord? We have here a tremendous event that moves in the context of history and is at the same time an invasion of history by the power of God. Men would not stake their lives on this event without some adequate reasons for knowing that they were not following an illusion. The first Christians were sure that the tomb was empty. But they did not base their faith on an empty tomb. When Mary Magdalene returns to the tomb after she has borne the message of the empty tomb to the disciples, she is still weeping and wondering where the body has been laid (John 20:11-13). Cleopas and his friend as they walk to Emmaus have heard the story of the empty tomb and also of the message of the angels that Jesus is alive, but they are still sad and discouraged men (Luke 24:17).

The belief in the resurrection of Jesus rested upon the fact that Jesus after his Passion manifested himself as alive to selected witnesses among his followers. These manifestations took place over a period of forty days. Paul in his letter to the Corinthians lists some of them. He mentions an appearance to Peter that is also referred to in Luke 24:34; an appearance to the twelve; an appearance to more than five hundred brethren at one time (this is mentioned only by Paul); an appearance to James, the Lord's brother;

and an appearance to all of the apostles. The list is not exhaustive. It is a summing up of that which was known by the Christian community. Paul follows this with his own personal testimony to the appearance of the risen Lord to him. He makes an additional reference to this in 1 Corinthians 9:1. These appearances were limited to the Christian community. They were given, as Peter says, "not to all the people but to us who were chosen by God as witnesses" (Acts 10:41). The Christian church was made up of those who had heard and believed the testimony of those who were chosen by God to be witnesses of the resurrection.

Supporting evidence of the way in which the knowledge of the resurrection is at the heart of the life of the early church is to be found in the mass of almost incidental references to it that are found in the New Testament. Consider, for example, Romans 1:4 and 8:11; 2 Corinthians 4:14; 1 Thessalonians 4:14; Hebrews 13:20; 1 Peter 1:3; and Revelation 1:18. Evidence is given also in 1 Corinthians 15:12 in the fact that those in Corinth who insisted that there was no resurrection of the dead did not question the fact of the resurrection of Jesus Christ. The knowledge of the resurrection of her Lord was an integral part of the knowledge which God committed to his church.

What was the bearing of this knowledge on the life of the church? Do we have here an isolated marvel or are we dealing with knowledge that affects the whole thought and life of the church? Paul in 1 Corinthians 15:12-19 looks at the implications for the life of the church that would follow if the belief in the resurrection of the Christ ceased to be a part of the faith of the church. For the sake of argument he is stating his positions in negative terms. But if we state his thought in positive terms we can get the full force of his statements. There was a group in Corinth which kept insisting that there was no such thing as the resurrection of the dead. Paul affirms that their philosophy is false because it is punctured by a fact. He knows that Christ is risen from the dead. In a similar manner we may find scholars today who have adopted a philosophy of life in which there is no room for the resurrection, or indeed for any activity of God. In her testimony to the resurrection the church affirms the fact of God's activity in history and insists that Christian proclamation must begin by pointing to that which God has done. In moments of doubt Paul himself faced the horror of having misrepresented God in giving his testimony to the fact that God raised up Christ. But in his heart he knows that this is not the case. He is confident that he and the apostles are true witnesses of God and that he has not called upon men to thrust forth their lives upon an illusion.

Paul insists that the Corinthians are no longer in their sins. By this he does not mean that they have all attained sinless perfection. A rapid glance at the subjects discussed in the Corinthian letter would leave us in no uncertainty concerning the reality of sin in the lives of the Corinthian converts. But the Corinthians know that there is no condemnation to those who are in Christ Jesus. They know that their sins have been forgiven and that they are accepted by God as his children. They know that they are walking by faith and are beginning to experience victory over sin.

Paul knows also that those who are asleep in Christ have not perished. In other places he spells out in more detail the Christian hope for those who die in the Lord. But this hope in all its forms is based on the assumption of a living Lord who is able to lead his people beyond death into the resurrection life of God.

In the King James Version, 1 Corinthians 15:19 reads: "If in this life only we have hope in Christ, we are of all men most miserable." In the Revised Standard Version it reads: "If in this life we who are in Christ have only hope, we are of all men most to be pitied."[1] The thought expressed in the King James translation is true. If there be a salvation for mankind, it must be a salvation that penetrates the supreme mystery of death. A salvation that dealt with our life in this world but gave us no hope for the life beyond the grave would leave us in an impossible position. But the Revised Standard translation is probably closer to the meaning of the Greek text. According to this translation, Paul says that if we who are Christians have *only hope,* we are of all men most to be pitied. If we are to give ourselves in full surrender to Jesus Christ we need more than the faint hope that there may be a life after death. We need some ground of confidence so that we can know that we are not venturing forth upon an illusion that will betray us in our time of need. And God has given us more than hope. He has sent his Son to us. He has brought again from the dead our Lord Jesus Christ, the great shepherd of the sheep, through the blood of the everlasting covenant (Hebrews 13:20). The Christ has manifested himself as alive to witnesses chosen by God. We have the testimony of these witnesses. We have the church that was called into being by this testimony. We have in our hearts the testimony of the Spirit to the truth of the gospel. We have hope, but we do not have only hope. We have a hope that is firmly based in the knowledge of what God has already done for us in Jesus Christ.

There was an anti-God rally in Russia in which the speaker poured ridicule on the Christian faith as the outworn creed of a bygone day. When he had finished and asked for comments, an old man rose and made his way slowly to the platform. He looked at the speaker and the audience and then gave expression to his faith as he cried out: "Christ is risen!" After a moment of silence there came back from the audience in thunderous tones the response: "He is risen! He is risen indeed!"

# IV

## THE LIMITATIONS OF KNOWLEDGE

*Scripture Background—1 Corinthians 13.*

"We know in part . . . now I know in part; but then shall I know even as also I am known."—1 Corinthians 13:9, 12 (K.J.V.).

Paul speaks here as a Christian, as one who has taken his stand with those who have heard the message of the gospel. In verse 12 he uses the pronoun "I" because he is giving expression to that which is his own conviction. But even here he speaks as a representative Christian. Paul expects those to whom he writes to identify themselves with him as he says, "Now I know in part; but then shall I know even as also I am known."

Paul's statement is first of all an affirmation of the reality of our knowledge. It may be necessary to say, "We know *in part.*" But in saying this we are also saying that there are some things that we do know. We do not live in a world in which we are skeptical of any knowledge that agrees with reality. We do not exist in a universe in which nothing can be known with certainty.

Deep in our hearts we know that there is a difference between right and wrong. We live in a world in which there is an eternal distinction between good and evil. We know that love is better than hate and that the truth is better than a lie. Apart from the insights of the Christian faith, there are some great certainties which we can use as a guide to conduct.

When we take our stand within the framework of the Christian faith, we find that there are certain great affirmations which we can and must make. God has made himself known to his people. He has not left them in complete ignorance of him and without any knowledge of his will for them. We need to place here some of the great affirmations of Paul. He writes to the Corinthians: "We know that 'an idol has no real existence,' and that 'there is no God but one.' For although there may be so-called gods in heaven or on earth—as indeed there are many 'gods' and many 'lords'—yet for us there is one God, the Father, from whom are all things and for whom we exist, and one Lord, Jesus Christ, through whom are all things and through whom we exist" (1 Corinthians 8:4-6). This is knowledge that has been committed to the Christian community. Paul realizes this as he adds: "However, not all possess this knowledge" (verse 7). Paul has made a tremendous affirmation, but he is confident that it is in agreement with reality.

He writes to the Romans: "We know that God worketh all things for good to those who love him,[2] to them who are called according to his purpose" (Romans 8:28). This is a philosophy of life that is highly debatable. But it is inevitable if we share Paul's understanding of the purpose of God at work with those whom he has called to bring about their glorification. The called are to be "conformed to the image of his Son . . . that he might be the first-born among many brethren" (Romans 8:29).

Paul encourages the Corinthians as he writes: "We know that if the earthly tent we live in is destroyed, we have a building from God, a house not made with hands, eternal in the heavens" (2 Corinthians 5:1). This is a tremendous expression of the hope of life after death. It does not seem impossible if we believe with Paul that Jesus died and rose again. In his debate with Peter in Antioch, Paul can appeal to knowledge which he and Peter hold in common when he says, "We . . . know that a man is not justified by works of the law but through faith in Jesus Christ" (Galatians 2:15-16). The knowledge of justification by faith alone was part of the heritage of the whole Christian community.

Paul's great affirmations of assured knowledge are not limited to passages in which he begins by saying, "We know." There are other places in which a body of knowledge is implied as the background of his statement. When he says, "Knowing the fear of the Lord, we persuade men" (2 Corinthians 5:11), he has just said, "We must all appear before the judgment seat of Christ, so that each one may receive good or evil, according to what he has done in the body" (2 Corinthians 5:10). The urgency of his persuading men is based on his knowledge that we must all appear before the judgment seat of Christ. Paul knows that we live in a moral order in which there is an inevitable relation between sowing and reaping. He can write to the Galatians: "Do not be deceived; God is not mocked, for whatever a man sows, that he will also reap" (Galatians 6:7). Christians do not live in a world in which nothing is known of God or of his will for man.

But while Paul would never have questioned the reality of the knowledge that had been given to the Christian community, he can also say, "We know *in part*." Our knowledge is imperfect and broken. There are some things we do know and there are many things we do not know. In some fields we have a limited knowledge which is true to the facts of life, but there is always a body of knowledge to which we have not yet attained.

This is true in the various fields of secular knowledge. Our boundaries of knowledge can be thought of in terms of the circumference of a circle. As we increase our knowledge we increase the circumference of the circle. But we also increase our awareness of the things we do not know that lie just beyond the range of the things we do know. The man who knows very little is apt to be cocky because he knows next to nothing of those vast areas of knowledge that are beyond him. The great scholar is usually humble in his assertions because he knows all too well the limits of his knowledge. The man who has given his life to the study of medicine knows many things which are not known by the ordinary layman. But he knows also that no one man can be an expert in all of the branches of knowledge that are associated with the study of medicine.

The field of knowledge is tremendous today. A generation ago it was thought that men knew most of what was to be known in the field of physics. With the discovery of atomic energy the area of knowledge to be explored in this field has been enlarged in a way that is hardly believable. Not all of the old knowledge is invalidated. But all of it has to be seen in its relation to the new things that have been discovered.

Paul is similar to the men of real scholarship in the various fields of human inquiry in his awareness of the limits of his knowledge. He marvels at the mystery of evil and in particular at the mystery of Israel's rejection of her Messiah. He is the apostle to the Gentiles. As the apostle to the Gentiles, he has seen men of Greek and Roman origin as they have turned to God and taken their place in the Christian church. He is thrilled that there was given to him as the least of all the saints the privilege of preaching "to the Gentiles the unsearchable riches of Christ" (Ephesians 3:8). But he cannot understand the rejection of Israel. As he closes the three chapters of Romans in which he faces the unbelief of Israel he writes: "O the depth of the riches and wisdom and knowledge of God! How *unsearchable* are his judgments and how *inscrutable* his ways! 'For who has known the mind of the Lord, or who has been his counselor?' " (Romans 11:33-34). There are many, many things which we cannot fully understand. We do not know why Mohammedanism was permitted to arise and to turn away from the Christian faith many of those who live in the lands in which Christianity had its origin. We do not know why our generation has had to struggle with an atheistic communism that has gained a dominant position over vast areas of our earth and has claimed the passionate loyalty of many millions.

In our more personal experiences we are constantly being faced with things we cannot understand. We do not know what to say when a friend goes down with cancer or when a person we love is hopelessly crippled in an automobile accident. We can understand Paul as he wrestles with his thorn in the flesh and prays for its removal, only to have his petition denied. We can identify with Milton when he wonders why blindness has come to him so as to make it seem impossible for him to continue to serve his God through the writing of poetry.

We can realize also that much of Christian knowledge has to be expressed in terms of symbols. Paul can speak of "a building from God, a house not made with hands, eternal in the heavens" (2 Corinthians 5:1). He can be confident of its existence, but he cannot give a positive description of it. We have to think of heaven in part in terms of the elimination of the negations of earth. We think of it as a place where some of the things we do not like here will not be found. As Christians we have some knowledge, but our knowledge is imperfect. We see through a glass darkly, and it is only in hope that we look forward to a time when we will see face to face.

It is in the midst of the imperfection of our knowledge that Paul reminds us of the fact that we are known. He says, "I know in part"; but he adds, "then shall I know even as also *I am known.*" The certainty of being known of God gives some confidence to the Christian in the midst of the uncertainties of life. He is sure that his life is in the hands of the God who knows him and loves him. We see this illustrated within the limits of our human experience. The parents of a very young child may find it necessary to take the child to the hospital for a serious operation. This can be a terrifying experience to the child. But if the parents stand beside the child in the whole of the experience, part of the terror is removed.

Jesus faced the mystery of his Passion with the words, "Shall I not drink the cup which the Father has given me?" (John 18:11). Christians can face the things that life brings them in the confidence that these experiences have come as part of the Father's will for them. As we face the mysteries of life there are times when we are not so much concerned to know the answer as to know that there is an answer. Job never received the answers to his questions, but he came to a knowledge of God which made it unnecessary for him to have the answers. When we have come to know the God who has made himself known in Jesus Christ we can leave many things to the mystery of his will. We can follow the advice of Peter and cast all our anxieties on him in the knowledge that he cares for us (1 Peter 5:7). In the midst of the imperfections of our knowledge we can know that we are known.

Paul knows that he knows in part, but he is confident that the time will come when he will know even as he is known. He believes that the time will come when he will be able to see the meaning of many of the things which he cannot understand now. We can face life's mysteries in the hope that when we have finished life's pilgrimage we will come to the time in which we know as we are known. As we live into the full meaning of the Christian faith we can begin to have in our life here some understanding of the mysteries of life. We can have foregleams of the fuller knowledge that is yet to come.

Perhaps Paul has overstated his case. We may never be able to know as we are known, because we are creatures and the One who knows us is the Creator. But we can hope to have in the life to come a perspective that is not possible in the life we know now. We will be able to see the life of earth in the light of heaven. We may never know the complete fulfillment of the prophecy "as for knowledge, it will pass away." We would hope to continue to explore the unsearchable riches of Christ. We can have the hope of a knowledge that answers our quest for knowledge and goes far beyond the knowledge that we can attain within the limitations of our earthly life.

# V

## ONE GOD—THE FATHER

*Scripture Background—1 Corinthians 8:1-7.*

"We know that 'an idol has no real existence,' and that 'there is no God but one.' . . . for us there is one God, the Father, from whom are all things and for whom we exist."—1 Corinthians 8:4, 6.

Paul flings off this text almost incidentally. He is in the midst of the discussion of whether Christians should eat meat offered to idols. This was a question of real concern to the Corinthian Christians. They knew that they could not participate in the idolatrous feasts of their pagan neighbors. But they were uncertain about whether when invited to the home of a friend who was not a Christian they could partake of meat that might have been offered to idols. This particular question does not concern us now.

Our concern with the passage is that as an aside spoken in the midst of his argument Paul makes a great affirmation concerning the knowledge of God that is to be found in the Christian community. He says that "an idol has no real existence" and that Christians know that "there is no God but one." He goes on to say that for us (that is, for the Christian community) "there is one God, the Father." As he points to this one God, the Father, Paul says that *from* him are all things and that *for* him we exist. He sets beside this one God, the Father, the one Lord Jesus Christ and says that *through* him are all things and that *through* him we exist. Having stated the knowledge of God that is found in the Christian community he hastens to add that "not all possess this knowledge" (1 Corinthians 8:7).

We have here some tremendous affirmations concerning God. We should notice that first of all there is a sweeping affirmation concerning the idols and the many gods of the non-Christian world.

Paul says that Christians know that an idol has no real existence. The more enlightened among the pagans did not think the idols had any real existence, but rather that the idol was an attempt to make an image of a god who did exist. The Christians said that the idols of the ancient world and the gods that they represented did not actually exist. They were creations of the minds of men. They had no actual existence. In this setting we can understand why the Christians were called atheists. They denied the existence of the gods their neighbors worshiped.

We need to pause here to realize that an illusion that is believed can profoundly affect the lives of those who believe it. To give a contemporary illustration, the emperor worship of Japan was used by the Japanese militarists to arouse among many of the people of Japan a mystical dedication to the belief in the destiny of Japan as ruler of the East. And Marxist communism with its deification of the class struggle has aroused on the part of many of its adherents a dedication to the establishment of world communism that has made them willing to suffer and die for this cause.

Paul goes on to say, "We know that . . . 'there is no God but one.'" This is an uncompromising statement of monotheism. In this Paul is making one of the great affirmations of Judaism. He may actually be quoting from the Shema (Deuteronomy 6:4). The Mohammedans would agree that there is only one God, but they would say that Mohammed is his prophet. It is not enough simply to affirm monotheism. We must be able to say what we know of this one God and point to the place at which he has made himself known. Paul defines his affirmation of monotheism when he says, "For us there is one God, the Father." How has Paul come to the knowledge of this one God, the Father?

At times in Christian theology men have advanced various arguments to attempt to prove the existence of God. They have looked at the created universe and have said that the very concept of the creature implies the existence of a Creator. They have looked at the presence of design in the structure of the universe and have said that the world around us points to an infinite Mind. They have looked at the sense of right and wrong in the consciences of man and have said that the very existence of the idea of obligation involves the existence of an Obligator. It is not our purpose here to develop or evaluate these and similar arguments. They do show that theism makes more sense than atheism, but they have the flaw of making man the certainty and God the uncertainty. The god who is found at the far end of a syllogism is too much of an abstraction to save the world.

All of these arguments would have been foreign to the thought processes of Paul and other writers of the Bible. The biblical writers never attempt to prove the existence of God. They do not have to, because their knowledge of God has come through encounter. The biblical writers point to the mighty acts of God. They start with the fact of revelation. They bear witness to the way in which God has made himself known.

Paul stands in the heritage of the knowledge of God that was found in Israel. But when he says, "For us there is one God, the Father," he is thinking of the knowledge of God to be found in the Christian community. This knowledge has come through encounter with Jesus Christ. Jesus has said: "All things have been delivered to me by my Father; and no one knows the Son except the Father, and no one knows the Father except the Son and any one to whom the Son chooses to reveal him" (Matthew 11:27).

Of this God, Paul in the passage before us makes two statements. He says that *from* him are all things. The one God who has made himself known to us in Jesus Christ is the source of all life. He is eternally the Father in his relation to the Son. He is also the Father in the sense that his loving care extends to the creatures he has made. His eye is on the sparrow and not one falls to the ground without his knowledge. He is peculiarly the Father in his relation to the human beings whom he has made in his own image.

As he thinks of this one God, Paul says also, ". . . for whom we exist." Man does not find the center of his being in himself. Man exists to glorify God. It is here that we realize the difference between being children of God by creation and children of God by redemption. Man as we know him is in rebellion against God. But God has come to man as Redeemer. This is the purpose of his coming in Jesus Christ, and those who respond to God's offer of love and mercy in Jesus Christ become spiritually the children of God.

Jesus spoke so intimately of the Father that when his disciples knew that the time had come for him to leave them Philip voiced the feeling of the group when he said, "Lord, show us the Father, and we shall be satisfied." Jesus said to him, "Have I been with you so long, and yet you do not know me, Philip? He who has seen me has seen the Father; how can you say, 'Show us the Father'? Do you not believe that I am in the Father and the Father in me?" (John 14:8-10).

In Jesus, the Father in heaven has made himself known to us in a person who has lived in the context of our earthly life. The attitudes of Jesus are the attitudes of the Father in heaven. The highest thing that we can say about the Father in heaven is that he is made known in the Son he has sent to us. John could write: "The Word became flesh and dwelt among us, full of grace and truth; we have beheld his glory, glory as of the only Son from the Father. . . . No one has ever seen God; the only Son, who is in the bosom of the Father, he has made him known" (John 1:14, 18). And Paul could write of Jesus: "He is the image of the invisible God" (Colossians 1:15).

The resurrection came as the consummation of the knowledge of God that is in Jesus Christ our Lord. This was the mighty act of God which was at the heart of the faith of the Christian community. The writer of the letter to the Hebrews brings his epistle to a close as he points his readers to the God who brought again from the dead our Lord Jesus Christ (Hebrews 13:20).

The knowledge of God which is found in Jesus Christ is not a knowledge of God which has come as the result of the searchings of man. This is the place at which God has taken the initiative and has come to man to make himself known in the context of the life of man. Between the God and Father of our Lord Jesus Christ and all the other "gods many and lords many" there is a profound difference. The God who has come to us in Christ is the one and only, the *true* and the *living* God. Paul reminds the Thessalonians that they turned from the worship of idols to serve the "living and true God" (1 Thessalonians 1:9). This God is the true God. He actually exists. The other gods are creations of the minds of men. But this God is the creator of man. He is the living God. He is the God who acts. The so-called gods cannot do anything. But this God can bring again from the dead the Lord Jesus Christ. He can act continually in history as he calls his church into being. This is the God who makes decisions concerning us. This is the God who determines our destiny.

How can modern man in the midst of his secularism and his unbelief come to the experience of encounter with this one God who has made himself known in Jesus Christ? The answer is that we cannot manipulate this experience. It is God himself who confronts men. It is God who calls us into his own kingdom and glory. But we can put ourselves in the place of encounter. We can read the New Testament as men who have ears to hear what this book has to say to us. We can let ourselves become involved in the life of some believing community where there are men and women to whom the sense of the presence of God is a reality. We can become acquainted with the history of the church in general and, in particular, with the lives of those whom God has used as the bearer of his message to men. We can listen to the testimony of these men to the place of the Christ in their lives. Most important of all, we can draw near to the place of encounter with the readiness to surrender our wills to the One who would come to us as Savior and Lord. If we will do this we may come to realize the truth of the hymn:

> I sought the Lord, and afterward I knew
> He moved my soul to seek Him, seeking me;
> It was not I that found, O Saviour true;
> No, I was found of Thee.[3]

There is a knowledge of God in the Christian community. Not all men possess this knowledge. It is a knowledge of God that is given to those who have heard the word that God has spoken to man in Jesus Christ. But in the words which precede our text Paul reminds us that knowledge as such is not enough. When we understand the revelation of God that is in Jesus Christ, the important question for us is not whether we know about God but whether God knows us; that is, whether he recognizes us as belonging to him. Knowledge apart from love can become the basis for arrogance. But if when we have encountered the God who has come to us in Christ we have responded in love, we can be confident that we are among those who are being called. Paul has written: "If one loves God, one is known by him" (1 Corinthians 8:3).

# VI

## ONE LORD—JESUS CHRIST

*Scripture Background—1 Corinthians 8:4-7.*

"For us there is . . . one Lord, Jesus Christ, through whom are all things and through whom we exist."—1 Corinthians 8:6.

When Paul as the spokesman for the Christian community says that for us there is one Lord Jesus Christ, through whom are all things and through whom we exist, he is giving expression to a very high view of Jesus Christ. He is affirming that a person who had lived in the context of our earthly society less than three decades before the time of the writing of the letter to the Corinthians is to be recognized as the one Lord, the agent of creation and the One through whom we all exist. Why did the early Christians think so highly of the Founder of their faith? The answer is that they were led to this affirmation of the full deity of their Lord by their sense of the authority of his teachings, by their knowledge of his mighty acts, by their understanding of his testimony as to *Who* he was, and by the testimony to him that was given to them by God the Father. The high view of Jesus Christ which is found in the Apostles' Creed and more particularly in the Nicene Creed is a faithful reflection of the testimony to him which is found in the New Testament. Paul is speaking for the whole community of faith of the New Testament when he writes: "There is one God, and there is *one mediator between God and men, the man Christ Jesus,* who gave himself as a ransom for all." He gives his personal relation to this as he adds: "the testimony to which was borne at the proper time. For this I was appointed a preacher and apostle (I am telling the truth, I am not lying), a teacher of the Gentiles in faith and truth" (1 Timothy 2:5-7).

The recognition of Jesus as a unique Person was involved in the knowledge which his contemporaries had of his mighty works. Nicodemus and his friends reached the conclusion that Jesus was a teacher sent from God because they knew no one could do the signs that Jesus did unless God was with him (John 3:2). When Jesus at Caesarea Philippi asked his disciples, "Who do men say that the Son of man is?" he received an answer which showed that all of his contemporaries recognized in him a Person who was unique, a Person who had to be explained in some unusual way. At this time, Peter as the spokesman for the disciples answered the question, "Who do you say that I am?" with the reply, "You are the Christ, the Son of the living God" (Matthew 16:13-17). This was a God-given insight of faith. Jesus accepted it as a true testimony to his deity.

A study of the testimony of Jesus to himself will lead inevitably to the conclusion that Jesus claimed in a unique sense to be the Son of God. His enemies fully recognized this when they said to Pilate, "We have a law, and by that law he ought to die, because he has made himself the Son of God" (John 19:7).

The witness to the resurrection was to those who received it the divine confirmation of the unique claims of Jesus. Peter could say to the Jerusalem mob: "This Jesus God raised up, and of that we all are witnesses." He could continue: "Let all the house of Israel *therefore* know assuredly that God has made him both Lord and Christ, this Jesus whom you crucified" (Acts 2:32, 36). Paul in the opening verses of the letter to the Romans says that Jesus was "designated Son of God in power according to the Spirit of holiness by his resurrection from the dead" (Romans 1:4).

Many of those who gave the New Testament witness were among the ones to whom Jesus had presented himself alive after his Passion "by many proofs, appearing to them during forty days, and speaking of the kingdom of God" (Acts 1:3). The New Testament Christians believed also in the ascension of Jesus. They thought of him as at the right hand of God (Acts 7:55-56). And these same Christians were conscious of the unseen but very real presence of Jesus with his people. The Christology of the New Testament was not something that the first Christians read into the facts. It was the view of Jesus that was inevitable when the testimony to him was heard and understood.

Our concern in this study is not so much to summarize the reasons which led the first Christians to affirm the full deity of Jesus Christ as it is to see the way in which they set Jesus, whom they acknowledged as the Lord, in his relation to the Father, to the created universe, and to the other "lords" of the ancient world. Paul in the passage before us begins by saying: "We know that 'an idol has no real existence,' and that 'there is no God but one.' " He continues: "For although there may be so-called gods in heaven or on earth—as indeed there are many 'gods' and many 'lords'—yet for us there is one God, the Father, from whom are all things and for whom we exist." We have here one of the greatest statements of monotheism to be found in the Scriptures. Paul sees nothing out of place in adding to this statement the words of our text, "and one Lord, Jesus Christ, through whom are all things and through whom we exist."

Many of the Jews found it difficult to accept the lordship of Jesus Christ because they were committed to monotheism and they felt that the acknowledgment of the deity of Jesus Christ violated their belief in the one God. Paul was deeply rooted in Judaism, but he does not hesitate to say that for the Christians there was one God, the Father, and one Lord Jesus Christ. The unity of the Godhead is affirmed in the fact that the Son does always that which is pleasing to the Father. Paul is convinced that the one God, the Father, is known as he makes himself known through the Son he has sent to us and that this knowledge becomes effective for us as it is brought home to us by the Holy Spirit.

Our text sees the one Lord Jesus Christ as he is the agent of creation. Paul is referring to Jesus Christ when he says: "through whom are all things and through whom we exist." This concept is stated in the prologue of John's Gospel as John writes: "In the beginning was the Word, and the Word was with God, and the Word was God. He was in the beginning with God; all things were made through him, and without him was not anything made that was made" (John 1:1-3). It is amazing that the New Testament writers should have thought so highly of a Person who had lived in their midst. But this is consistently their testimony. And this testimony is peculiarly interesting in a world in which our concept of the created universe is being vastly enlarged. The book of Colossians is often studied for its testimony to Jesus Christ as the Creator. It is here that Paul writes of the Son: "In him all things were created, in heaven and on earth, visible and invisible, whether thrones or dominions or principalities or authorities—all things were created through him and for him. He is before all things, and in him all things hold together" (Colossians 1:16-17). The language of Colossians is one of the great statements of the New Testament, but it merely makes explicit that which is implicit in the words of our text. The language of the Nicene Creed supports Paul's concept of Jesus Christ as Creator when it refers to him as the one "by whom all things were made."

In Browning's Epistle of Karshish, he has the Arab physician write of Lazarus:

> This man so cured regards the curer, then,
> As—God forgive me! who but God himself,
> Creator and sustainer of the world,
> That came and dwelt in flesh on it awhile!
> —'Sayeth that such an one was born and lived,
> Taught, healed the sick, broke bread at his own house,
> Then died, with Lazarus by, for aught I know,
> And yet was . . . what I said nor choose repeat,
> And must have so avouched himself, in fact,
> In hearing of this very Lazarus.[4]

Paul expresses the faith of the early Christian community when he says that they recognized in the One who lived among them the Creator of the world and the Person to whom they owed their existence. The meaning for us of the belief in the incarnation is expressed by Browning in the closing words of the Epistle of Karshish in which the Arab physician says:

> The very God! think, Abib; dost thou think?
> So, the All-Great, were the All-Loving too—
> So, through the thunder comes a human voice

Saying, "O heart I made, a heart beats here!
Face, my hands have fashioned, see it in myself!
Thou hast no power nor mayst conceive of mine,
But love I gave thee, with myself to love,
And thou must love me who have died for thee!"[5]

When the first Christians said, "Indeed there are . . . many
'lords'—yet for us there is . . . one Lord, Jesus Christ," they
were confessing a faith in Jesus Christ which made it impossible
for them to acknowledge any other lordship as superior to that of
the one Lord Jesus Christ. It was not long before this confession of
faith was tested. The Romans were on the whole quite tolerant of
the various religions found among the conquered peoples of the
Roman empire. They made no effort to enforce uniformity of
religion. But as a test of the loyalty of their subjects to the Roman
empire they did set up a pattern of emperor worship in which they
asked all the people of the empire to go through the form of offering
worship to the Emperor. This was supposed to be a bond of unity
within the diversities of the Roman empire. Most of the peoples of
the empire did not object to this. It meant for them simply adding
one more god to the pantheon of gods which they worshiped. The
Christians refused. They knew that the offering of homage to the
Emperor meant the denial of the one Lord Jesus Christ. They were
stubborn in their refusal. They were prepared to go to prison or to
death rather than to pour out a libation of oil or wine to the
Emperor. To their enemies this seemed to be a foolish point to be
stubborn about, but to the Christians it was a question of first
loyalty. It was because of the refusal of Christians to participate in
this type of offering to the Emperor that Christianity became a
forbidden religion, punished by death in the Roman empire.

The issue of emperor worship as a test of loyalty to the state was
revived in recent years in the worship of the Emperor in Japan.
Christians in the Japanese empire had to face the same question that
the first Christians faced. Many of them accepted persecution rather
than to acquiesce in a worship that was to them idolatry. The same
issue in a somewhat different form is present today when Christian
communities seek to exist in communist lands. The Christians can-

not affirm the atheism of the communist state. They cannot avow a loyalty to the principles of Karl Marx which would take precedence over their acknowledgment of the one Lord Jesus Christ.

The issue appears in another form in the various efforts at religious syncretism which we face in the world today. Christianity is in encounter on a world scale with the other faiths of mankind. Efforts are being made to have Christians enter upon some form of religious syncretism in which they recognize the other faiths of mankind as valid roads to the knowledge of God. Christians are accused of being narrow and arrogant in insisting that their faith in which God has come to man in Jesus Christ is the one and only road to God. Here again the confession of the one Lord Jesus Christ prevents the Christians from entering upon a road of compromise in which they tone down the absolute claims of their faith.

It is an empty gesture for Christians to say, "For us there is one Lord, Jesus Christ," without seeking to enter on a road of obedience in which Jesus Christ actually becomes the lord of their lives. The Christian life is life under the lordship of Jesus Christ. It is not always possible for us to know the full meaning of the acknowledgment of Jesus as Lord in all the various areas of life. But a beginning must be made. Christians may properly differ in their understanding of the will of God for them in race relations. But they cannot debate the thesis that the church takes the pattern of her life from her Lord and not from the prevailing patterns of the society around her.

Christians may differ in their patterns of the getting and spending of money. But they must agree in acknowledging that the lordship of Christ over their lives includes his lordship of their possessions. They must seek to use their possessions in a way that is pleasing to their Lord.

The patterns of life in our complex industrial society are not simple, and it is not always easy for Christians to spell out with clarity the implications of the lordship of Christ in the various areas of their lives. But the attempt must be made, and Christians must be known not only as the people of a faith in the one Lord Jesus Christ but as the people who are walking in the way of life which their Lord set forth. They must become the people of the Way.

# VII

## ONE HOLY SPIRIT—THE COUNSELOR

*Scripture Background—Galatians 4:1-7; 5:16-25.*

"God has sent the Spirit of his Son into our hearts . . ."—Galatians 4:6.

If you had asked the first Christians what was the most unique thing about their fellowship they would probably have said that they were the community of those who had received the Holy Spirit. While we do not find the idea expressed in any one sentence which begins with the words "we know," we are profoundly true to the thought of Paul when we say that the New Testament Christians knew themselves to be the community that the Holy Spirit had called into being. Paul speaks for the church of the New Testament when he says, "God has sent the Spirit of his Son into our hearts." In another setting he writes: "By one Spirit we were all baptized into one body" (1 Corinthians 12:13). It is clear also that when Paul says God has sent the *Spirit of his Son,* he is referring to the Holy Spirit. (In actual practice we do not need to distinguish between the consciousness of the living Lord with his people—unseen but not unreal—and the consciousness of the indwelling of the Holy Spirit in our hearts. It is the work of the Holy Spirit to lead us to the consciousness of the living Lord.)

It was in the experience of the coming of the Holy Spirit at Pentecost that the church of the New Testament became separated from the Israel according to the flesh. The risen Lord had told his disciples to tarry in Jerusalem until they were "clothed with power from on high" (Luke 24:49). In the great closing discourses recorded in the Gospel of John, Jesus had predicted the coming of the Counselor (John 16:4-15). At Pentecost the Spirit came upon the band of disciples as they were at prayer in an upper room. In the power of the Spirit, they went out and gave their testimony. The Spirit brought the truth of their message home to the hearts of those to whom they spoke, and there were added to the church that day around three thousand persons (Acts, chapter 2). The coming of the Spirit was crucial when the message of the gospel was carried from Jerusalem to Samaria. When Peter and John prayed for those who had been baptized and laid their hands upon them, the Holy Spirit fell upon them (Acts 8:14-17). And the coming of the Holy Spirit was decisive when the gospel was first preached to Gentiles. Peter under the guidance of the Holy Spirit went to Caesarea and preached to the Gentiles who were assembled in the home of Cornelius. As he extended to them the offer of forgiveness of sins through the name of Jesus, the Spirit fell on the audience and Peter marveling said, "Can any one forbid water for baptizing these people who have received the Holy Spirit just as we have?" (Acts 10:47). His reference to the coming of the Holy Spirit at Caesarea silenced all criticism when he reported his action to the apostles and the brethren who were in Judea (Acts 11:18).

The understanding of the church as the community of those who had received the Spirit is involved in Paul's experience with a group of disciples he found in Ephesus. He puts to them the question: "Did you receive the Holy Spirit when you believed?" They reply, "No, we have never even heard that there is a Holy Spirit." And Paul asks, "Into what then were you baptized?" They answer, "Into John's baptism." Paul led them through the testimony of John to the story of the One to whom John pointed. When they were baptized in the name of Jesus, "the Holy Spirit came on them; and they spoke with tongues and prophesied" (Acts 19:2-6).

We should notice in this connection that there were in the beginning certain visible signs which usually accompanied the coming of the Spirit. These included such things as speaking with tongues or prophesying. But the reality of the coming of the Spirit was the sense of the presence of God in the heart. Jesus came as God manifest in the flesh. The Holy Spirit comes as God present in the heart. This coming could be marked by visible signs, but it could be the quiet consciousness of the response of faith to the proclamation of the gospel. Paul could write to the Romans: "You are in the Spirit, if the Spirit of God really dwells in you." And he could add, "Any one who does not have the Spirit of Christ does not belong to him" (Romans 8:9).

In the verses which precede our text in Galatians, Paul has set forth the work of redemption which God has accomplished in the sending of his Son. At a time of his own choosing, God sent forth his Son born of woman, born under the law. The purpose of his coming was to redeem those who were under the law, that they might receive adoption as sons. This was an objective work of redemption wrought out by God in Christ. But how does the knowledge of this redemption come to the heart of the sinner? Paul answers this question as he writes: "And because you are sons, God has sent the Spirit of his Son into our hearts, crying, 'Abba! Father!'" "Abba" is the Aramaic word for Father. God has sent the Holy Spirit into our hearts, crying, "Father, Father!" When a man has adopted a son, we can see him bending over the infant boy and whispering, "Say Father, Father." In a similar way the God who has completed the work of redemption in Christ sends the Holy Spirit into our hearts, crying, "Father, Father!"

This work of the Holy Spirit is crucial because the Spirit takes the objective work of redemption and makes it vital in our experience. Paul writes in Romans, "When we cry, 'Abba! Father!' it is the Spirit himself bearing witness with our spirit that we are children of God" (Romans 8:15b-16). Paul, Timothy, and Silas went to Thessalonica and preached the gospel in this Greek city. Later Paul writes from Corinth to the Thessalonians: "We know, brethren beloved by God, that he has chosen you; for our gospel came to you not only in word, but also in power and in the Holy Spirit and with full conviction" (1 Thessalonians 1:4-5). The good news which Paul preached in Thessalonica was delivered in words. But the gospel came also in power. The Thessalonian Christians heard it and believed it with such full conviction that they were willing to suffer for their faith. Paul is telling us that the gospel came with full conviction because the Holy Spirit brought the message home to those who received it. In 1 Corinthians 12:3 he writes: "No one can say 'Jesus is Lord' except by the Holy Spirit."

This understanding of the work of the Holy Spirit was necessary in the world in which Paul lived. It is equally necessary in the modern world. The message of the gospel cuts across many of the categories of modern thought. If it is to be received with full conviction—the conviction that men can live by and die by—it must be that the Spirit who speaks through the preacher testifies to the truth of the message in the hearts of those that hear it. All Christian preaching should be ventured upon in the hope that the Holy Spirit will honor the message and make it the vehicle of his testimony in the hearts of those who hear it.

The Holy Spirit does not bring us to the knowledge that we are children of God and then leave us to make our way alone in the pilgrimage of faith. A mother making her prayer for her newborn son concludes her prayer with the sentence, "Lord, I would walk with him part of the way." The mother knows that she probably will not be able to walk with her son all of the way, but she wants to walk with him part of the way that she may help him get started in life. When the Holy Spirit has brought us to the acknowledgment of Jesus as Lord, he does more than walk with us part of the way. He walks with us as the Spirit of God present in our hearts for the whole of the way.

In one form or another the struggle with evil is with us in the whole of our earthly pilgrimage. There are the temptations of childhood and youth. There are the greater temptations of middle age. And probably the most difficult period of life for us to live through creatively is the time of retirement as it moves into the period of old age. We face the sins of the flesh as we are tempted to become slaves to drink or to some habit-forming drug. We face the struggle for purity in the midst of the desires that are part of our sex life. We experience the temptation to lives of selfishness or of indifference. We find it hard to keep the serenity of our spirit in the midst of the infirmities of old age. But as Christians we do not face the pilgrimage of life alone. God has sent the Holy Spirit into our hearts. Our bodies are the temple of the Holy Spirit. The Spirit is called the Paraclete—that is, the one who is called alongside of us. He is called the Comforter—the one who comforts us in sorrow and gives us strength for the demands that life makes upon us. He is called the Counselor—the one who guides us into the knowledge of the will of God for us. The epistles of Paul are saturated with references of this kind to the work of the Holy Spirit. And Paul is confident that if we will walk by the Spirit we will begin to see the fruits of the Spirit. He writes to the Galatians: "The fruit of the Spirit is love, joy, peace, patience, kindness, goodness, faithfulness, gentleness, self-control" (Galatians 5:22-23).

The Spirit does not leave us when we have come to the end of our earthly pilgrimage. Paul says that the Spirit's presence with us is our guarantee that we shall receive the eternal inheritance to which we have been called. The gift of the Spirit is the earnest of our inheritance. When a man closes a deal and makes a major payment, the money he has paid is proof of his intention to complete the payments. Paul is confident that sonship means also inheritance. We have quoted the passage in Romans in which he says, "The Spirit himself [is] bearing witness with our spirit that we are children of God." He follows this with the statement: "and if children, then heirs, heirs of God and fellow heirs with Christ, provided we suffer with him in order that we may also be glorified with him" (Romans 8:17). In the passage in which our text is found, Paul follows the statement that God has sent the Spirit of his Son into our hearts crying, "Abba! Father!" with the statement: "So through God you are no longer a slave but a son, and if a son then an heir" (Galatians 4:7).

In at least three places Paul points to the gift of the Spirit as the guarantee of our receiving the inheritance of the children of God. He writes to the Corinthians: "God . . . has put his seal upon us and given us his Spirit in our hearts as a guarantee" (2 Corinthians 1:21-22). In the same letter, in the fifth chapter, he writes: "We sigh with anxiety . . . that what is mortal may be swallowed up by life." He continues: "He who has prepared us for this very thing is God, who has given us the Spirit as a guarantee" (2 Corinthians 5:4-5). Because he knows the Spirit as a guarantee, he can say, "We are always of good courage" (2 Corinthians 5:6). He knows that to be absent from the body is to be at home with the Lord. In the same way, Paul writes to the Ephesians: "You also, who have heard the word of truth, the gospel of your salvation, and have believed in him, were sealed with the promised Holy Spirit, which is the guarantee of our inheritance until we acquire possession of it, to the praise of his glory" (Ephesians 1:13-14).

In the verses which precede our text, we have the statement of God's sending forth of his Son to be born of woman, and to accomplish the work of redemption. Paul knew that God's sending of his Son was the proof that God intended to carry out to completion the work of redemption which he had started at such great cost. He could write to the Romans: "He who did not spare his own Son but gave him up for us all, will he not also give us all things with him?" (Romans 8:32). While this argument is sound, it is based on something that is outside of me. But when God sends the Spirit of his Son to live in my heart I have in my own life an earnest of my ultimate redemption. The God who through his Spirit has called me to be his child is the God who has promised me that I will lay hold of the inheritance of the children of God. In the response of faith which the Holy Spirit has enabled me to make I have in my own life the earnest of my inheritance. We can close with the closing words of Paul to the Thessalonians: "He who calls you is faithful, and he will do it" (1 Thessalonians 5:24). To this promise we can add the words of the apostolic benediction. "The grace of the Lord Jesus Christ and the love of God and the *fellowship of the Holy Spirit* be with you all" (2 Corinthians 13:14).

# VIII

## THE REALITY OF EVIL

*Scripture Background—Romans 7:7—8:17.*

"We know that the law is spiritual; but I am carnal, sold under sin."—Romans 7:14.
"Let us . . . walk by the Spirit."—Galatians 5:25.

There is a sense in which some of the statements of Paul in the seventh chapter of Romans sound like the confessions of a tortured soul. He writes: "I do not understand my own actions. For I do not do what I want, but I do the very thing I hate" (Romans 7:15). He continues: "I know that nothing good dwells within me, that is, in my flesh. I can will what is right, but I cannot do it. For I do not do the good I want, but the evil I do not want is what I do" (Romans 7:18-19).

In these and similar expressions Paul speaks for himself and for all mankind. We all know the experience of seeing the good and approving it and then finding to our disgust that we do the evil. We all know that our ideals go beyond our deeds and that we do not live up to the creeds we profess. We can identify with the statements in the Book of Common Prayer of the Episcopal Church which read: "We have left undone those things which we ought to have done; And we have done those things which we ought not to have done; And there is no health in us."[6]

The story is told of a French preacher who, while lecturing on the seventh chapter of Romans to an audience in which Louis XIV was present, described the good man and the bad man in the Apostle Paul. He said that in the great apostle there were two men. One man saw the good and approved it and wanted to do it, but the other man turned from the vision of the good to the doing of the evil. According to the story, the king interrupted the preacher to say: "How well I know those two men. Not only were there two men in Paul, there are two men in Louis the Fourteenth." To this the preacher replied: "True, O King, but one of these men must die." The struggle between good and evil goes on in every human soul.

We should not deplore this. It is part of the worry and the wonder of being human. One of the things that distinguish the man from the beast is that there is in man the capacity to know good and evil. And with this knowledge there is some capacity for choice between right and wrong. No man is so depraved that he does not have at times glimmerings of the concept of the good and some sense of his capacity for responsible decisions.

Browning had an understanding of the necessity for this struggle in man, and with it a beginning of an understanding of the place of evil in the world that God has made. He writes:

> For me
> (Patience, beseech you!) knowledge can but be
> Of good by knowledge of good's opposite—
> Evil,—since, to distinguish wrong from right,
> Both must be known in each extreme, beside—
>
> . . . . . . .
>
> Type needs antitype:
> As night needs day, as shine needs shade, so good
> Needs evil: how were pity understood
> Unless by pain?[7]

Browning could not solve the mystery of evil, but he could see the place of struggle within the human soul. Bishop Blougram says:

> No, when the fight begins within himself,
> A man's worth something. God stoops o'er his head,
> Satan looks up between his feet— both tug—
> He's left, himself, i' the middle: the soul wakes
> And grows. Prolong that battle through his life!
> Never leave growing till the life to come![8]

The struggle between good and evil is present in some sense in every human being. But it is where the law of the Lord is recognized as a moral code which confronts them that men become most keenly conscious of the chasm between what they are and what they ought to be. Paul stood in the heritage of Judaism. He recognized the authority of the law which was the rule of life for his people. When Paul thinks of the law he may be thinking of the Ten Commandments as given through Moses and as containing a summary of the moral law. The great prophets had judged the fidelity of Israel to the covenant relation in terms of obedience to the Ten Commandments as the will of the Lord for his people. But when Paul thinks of the law he is thinking also of the whole pattern of commandments and ordinances which were part of the heritage of Judaism. The Christian could go beyond this and think in similar terms of "the commandments of Jesus."

In spite of the fact that the great controversy of his life was with those who would say to the Christians that unless they kept the law of Moses they could not be saved, Paul never speaks in disparaging terms of the law as it was given to Israel. He speaks for the New Testament community when he says, "We know that the law is spiritual" (Romans 7:14). He writes: "The law is holy, and the commandment is holy and just and good" (Romans 7:12). He could have joined with the writer of the 119th Psalm in his praise of the law of the Lord. Paul knew that the law was the expression of the will for man of a holy and righteous God.

Paul understood the law of the Lord not merely as an external code to which men must conform their actions but also as a way of life demanding purity of thought and motive. He would undoubtedly have been in sympathy with Jesus when in the Sermon on the Mount he deepened the Ten Commandments by applying them to the thoughts of the heart. Jesus insists that we must go beyond refraining from murder and deal with hate in the heart. He says that the man who looks upon a woman to lust after her has committed adultery with her already in his heart. The cherishing of lustful thoughts is a sin in kind if not in degree with the sin of adultery. Paul realizes that when the tenth commandment condemns the sin of covetousness the law reaches beyond the realm of external deeds into the whole area of the dominating desires of the heart. He felt that he might have kept the letter of the law, but he knew that he could not be completely free from covetous desires (Romans 7:7).

In the law of the Lord, man finds himself confronted with a moral code which sets forth the duty which God requires of man. Human beings who have this law are infinitely better off than those people who live in a land "where there aren't no Ten Commandments"[9] and there is nothing to control the lusts of men. But the intensity of moral struggle is felt most keenly where the law of the Lord is known. This is because the violation of the law of the Lord is correctly understood as sin against God. The Westminster Shorter Catechism defines sin as "any want of conformity unto, or transgression of, the law of God."[10]

Paul knows that through the law there comes knowledge of sin. There is of course some knowledge of good and evil apart from man's knowledge of the law in which God has made known his will for man. But Paul feels that if it had not been for the law, he would not have known sin (Romans 7:7). It is in the light of the law that sin becomes exceeding sinful. In this setting, sin is seen not merely as a failure to attain our own ideals or as a wrong to our brothers; sin is seen as disobedience to God and as deserving the wrath of a holy and righteous God. The knowledge of the law brings men to conviction of sin.

There is a limited sense in which the law incites to sin. There is in man at times a certain stubbornness in which he delights in doing the thing he is told not to do. Would Eve have eaten the apple in the garden if it had not been "forbidden fruit"? Man in his rebellion against God expresses his sense of revolt in an arrogance in which he scorns the law of the Lord and secretly believes that he can sin with impunity.

While Paul believes that the law is holy and just and good, he repudiates the keeping of the law as a way of salvation for mankind. Man cannot be saved by keeping the law because he cannot keep it perfectly. We cannot find salvation by an exalted ethical code because the more fully we understand the meaning of that code the more certain we are that we cannot keep it. Paul had sought to find salvation in this way. But he knew that through obedience to law he had not found acceptance with God. This failure to find salvation through the keeping of the law of Moses is a failure that is experienced in any attempt to find salvation through the keeping of an external code. Men have known a similar sense of failure when they have interpreted religion in terms of obedience to the commands of Jesus or in imitation of the way of life which Jesus lived.

Paul knows that the law is spiritual. This is one of the "we knows" of Paul. This is an abiding insight of the New Testament church as that church refused to repudiate the heritage of Israel. But Paul has a knowledge of himself that he must set side by side with his knowledge of the law. He expresses this when he says, "I am carnal, sold under sin." When Paul says, "I am carnal," he could mean, "I am flesh." We are spirits, but we are embodied spirits. There is a certain frailty to the flesh. Jesus recognized this when he said to the disciples who had fallen asleep in the Garden of Gethsemane: "Watch and pray that you may not enter into temptation; the spirit indeed is willing, but the flesh is weak" (Matthew 26:41). But the trouble with us is not that we are flesh in the sense that we know the frailty that is characteristic of all human beings. When Paul says, "I am carnal," he really means, "I am evil." He knows that there is in him a pull toward evil which means that although he can see the good and approve it, he finds that he does the evil. Jesus recognizes this when he describes his disciples with the phrase "You then, *who are evil*" (Matthew 7:11). Paul can say: "I know that nothing good dwells within me, that is, in my flesh. I can will what is right, but I cannot do it" (Romans 7:18). He continues: "I find it to be a law [law here means a consistent principle of action] that when I want to do right, evil lies close at hand. For I delight in the law of God, in my inmost self, but I see in my members another law at war with the law of my mind and making me captive to the law of sin which dwells in my members" (Romans 7:21-23).

Paul speaks here for himself and for the human race. There is a principle of evil at work in us which means that when we want to do right, evil lies close at hand. Even in our highest moments we are never completely free from sin. All too frequently we see the good but do the evil. We hate the things that we do, but we continue to do them.

We find ourselves in slavery to sin. This is what Paul means when he says, "I am . . . sold under sin." We find ourselves the victims of evil habits that we cannot break. We make the wrong decisions and make a mess out of our lives. We have ideals, but we cannot live up to them. We know that there is a kingdom of God, but we live in the kingdom of evil. We cry out with Paul, "Wretched man that I am! Who will deliver me from this body of death?" (Romans 7:24).

If Paul knows that he is "carnal, sold under sin," he knows also that he has found the Savior. The deliverance which Jesus brings is first of all deliverance from the attempt to find salvation through obedience to an external code. Paul knows that there is no condemnation to those who are in Christ Jesus. He knows that men are accepted with God not on the basis of what they have done or of what they are, but on the basis of what God has done for them in Christ. It is this that delivers us from the intolerable position of trying to lay hold of salvation through the keeping of the law.

Paul knows also that God has given his Holy Spirit to those who are Christ's. The Spirit is God present with us. The pull toward evil is still with us, but we have also the promptings of the Spirit. And with the Spirit of God at work in our hearts it is possible for us to begin to live in obedience to the leading of the Spirit. If we walk by the Spirit we will not yield to the suggestions of evil that come to us.

In the power of the Spirit we can begin to live as children of God. A woman may find herself in a home situation which leaves much to be desired. She may not be able to change the context of her life, but she can seek to walk by the Spirit in the life situation which she actually faces. A businessman may have the difficult task of trying to live as a Christian in the world of business in which he must move. An older person may face the challenge of living victoriously in the midst of the frailties and infirmities of old age. For each person in his life situation there is the call to holiness—the call to live as a child of God in the midst of his relationships and responsibilities. But the Christian faces life in the consciousness that he is not alone. The Spirit of God is with him in life's pilgrimage. He is called to live by the Spirit and to walk by the Spirit. The law remains as an expression of the will of God and as his guide in life's decisions. And the Spirit of God is with him to enable him to be adequate to the demands that life makes upon him. In such a situation a man can find the strength to walk by the Spirit until the fruits of the Spirit begin to appear in his life. Those who belong to Christ can lay hold of the power to crucify the flesh with its passions and desires.

# IX

## SALVATION BY FAITH ALONE

*Scripture Background—Galatians 2:11-16.*

"We . . . know that a man is not justified by works of the law but through faith in Jesus Christ."—Galatians 2:15-16.

The words of this text were spoken by Paul as part of his rebuke of Peter at the time of Peter's visit to the church at Antioch. They are Paul's appeal to an article of the Christian faith that was accepted both by Peter and by Paul. It was the knowledge that a man was saved not by what he was or by what he did but through faith —that is, through his acceptance of that which God had done for him in Jesus Christ.

Paul's setting of this "we know" as decisive in the debate between him and Peter at Antioch is of abiding significance. In the days immediately following Pentecost, the first Christians preached the gospel to Jews only. Christianity was a movement within the larger framework of Judaism. This pattern began to break when Philip preached the gospel in Samaria. But some of the Samaritans were descendants of the people of Northern Israel. The Samaritans had the law of Moses and a temple. It might have been possible to include them without moving out to the Gentile world. The pattern was decisively breached when Peter under the guidance of the Holy Spirit preached the gospel to Cornelius and his Italian friends at Caesarea. But we do not hear of a mass movement of Gentiles into the church at Caesarea. It was at Antioch that the Gentiles began to enter the church in large numbers. This work was begun by unknown preachers from Cyprus and Cyrene. It became so significant that the apostles sent Barnabas down to investigate it. Barnabas was so deeply impressed with what he saw that he stayed at

Antioch to lead the movement. After a brief time he realized that he needed help and went to Tarsus for Saul. The two men labored together in building in Antioch a Christian community which was made up of both Jews and Gentiles. Within the life of this church a believing community came into being in which the deep-seated division between Jew and Gentile was transcended.

When Peter came to Antioch he fitted quietly into the life of the church and made no distinction between Jews and Gentiles. This had been his accepted pattern of life in his missionary travels. But when some Jewish Christians came to Antioch from Jerusalem, Peter altered his manner of life to avoid giving them offense. These Christian Jews belonged to what was called the party of the circumcision. They had believed in Jesus as the Christ the Son of God and had put their faith in him as their Savior from sin. But they still believed in the necessity of circumcision, in the keeping of the laws of Moses, and in particular in observing the dietary laws of Judaism. They decided to eat at a table to themselves. Peter joined them. The other Jews followed Peter's example, and even Barnabas, impressed by the example of Peter, began to eat with them instead of with the Gentiles.

It was in this setting that Paul said to Peter: "If you, though a Jew, live like a Gentile and not like a Jew, how can you compel the Gentiles to live like Jews? We ourselves, who are Jews by birth and not Gentile sinners, yet who know that a man is not justified by works of the law but through faith in Jesus Christ, even we have believed in Christ Jesus, in order to be justified by faith in Christ, and not by works of the law, because by works of the law shall no one be justified" (Galatians 2:14-16).

Paul appeals here to the doctrine of salvation by faith alone to support his insistence that the Gentiles must be received in the church on terms of complete equality. It is interesting to notice that Peter makes exactly the same appeal at the Jerusalem Council in his speech to support the right of the Gentiles to be received without the added burden of circumcision and the keeping of the law of Moses. Of his Gentile converts at Caesarea, Peter says: "And God who knows the heart bore witness to them, giving them the Holy Spirit just as he did to us; and he made no distinction between us and them, but cleansed their hearts by faith. . . . we believe that we shall be saved through the grace of the Lord Jesus, just as they will" (Acts 15 :8-9, 11).

What is the relation between the doctrine of salvation by faith alone and the right of all men to be received in terms of equality in the Christian community? The relation is so simple that we are apt not to get it. If the Jew is saved, he is saved by faith alone. If the Gentile is saved, he is saved by faith alone. And because they have both come by faith alone, the distinctions of the secular world cannot have validity for them as they stand together in the believing community of the church. This is the reason that the Christian community can never be at peace with a pattern of segregation in which people are accepted or rejected in the church on the basis of such things as racial inheritance, class distinction, or economic status.

Paul was tremendously concerned at this point, because he was the apostle to the Gentiles. He knew that the Gentiles would not continue to come into the church unless they were certain that within the inner life of the church they were fully accepted. But Paul's main concern was not a matter of strategy; he was supremely concerned over the question of the acceptance of the Gentiles because he knew that the truth of the gospel was at stake.

Karl Barth in his *Theological Existence To-day!* sets forth a number of reasons for his rejection of the "German Christian Movement," which at the time of his writing of this pamphlet was seeking to dominate the Christian church in Germany. In the sixth of the eight reasons which he gives, he writes: "The fellowship of those belonging to the Church is not determined by blood, therefore, not by race, but by the Holy Spirit and Baptism. If the German Evangelical Church excludes Jewish Christians, or treats them as of a lower grade, she ceases to be a Christian Church."[11] We quickly approve this fearless defense of the right of the Christian Jews in Germany to full acceptance in the German Evangelical Church at a time when it was dangerous to utter sentiments like this in Hitler's Germany. But we have only to change a few words in the last sentence to make it read: "If the American Protestant Church excludes Negro Christians, or treats them as of a lower grade, she ceases to be a Christian Church." The right of men of different races to full acceptance in the Christian church is an inevitable implication of the central doctrine of salvation by faith alone. In defending the right of the Gentile Christians to be received without discrimination in the inner life of the Christian church in Antioch, Paul is defending the right of all men to be received into the fellowship of a Christian church if they meet the God-given conditions of church membership. He is basing his defense on the fact that he and Peter and the Gentile sinners have come into the church by the same road—that is, by faith in Jesus Christ. And Karl Barth is saying that the very existence of the church as a Christian community may be determined by her remembering that the fellowship of those belonging to the church is not determined by blood, therefore not by race, but by the Holy Spirit and by baptism.

But it would be a mistake to hear Paul's affirmation of justification by faith alone and to think only of the bearing of this doctrine on the question of segregation within the inner life of the church. Paul's message is directed to all those who are tempted to find salvation apart from faith and faith alone. We might paraphrase his message to Peter as follows: "Peter, you and I are not Gentile sinners. We are Jews. We were born within the family of God, but we had to learn that we had to believe in Christ in order to be justified by faith in Christ and not by works of the law." This came the hard way to Paul. He tells us in a biographical passage in Philippians that he had everything a man might hope to have in order to seek salvation through works. He was "circumcised on the eighth day, of the people of Israel, of the tribe of Benjamin, a Hebrew born of Hebrews; as to the law a Pharisee, as to zeal a persecutor of the church, as to righteousness under the law blameless" (Philippians 3:5-6). But Paul found that he had to give up confidence in all these things and put his faith in that which God had done for him in Christ. He had to count all of these things as refuse that he might gain Christ. It was through faith in Christ that he found the righteousness of God that depends on faith. It was through this experience that he began to know Christ, to know the power of his resurrection, to enter into the fellowship of his suffering, and to lay hold of the hope of the resurrection from the dead. The destruction of the confidence in the flesh of the self-righteous Pharisee is accomplished when the only thing that God can do for him is to send his Son to die for his sins.

One of the tragedies of life is that many things which are good in themselves may become the means of a confidence which keeps us from putting our trust in Christ and Christ alone. But Paul insists that by the works of the law no human being can ever be justified. Those who stand in a position of privilege must learn that it is through faith and faith alone that they find their way into the kingdom of God.

What, then, is the place of good works if they can never be the basis of salvation? We may illustrate this by an example that moves in the realm of human love. A man responds to the love of a woman and they move out together in the experience of marriage. In that experience he will do many things for her. (She also will do many things for him.) He will provide for her food, shelter, clothing, and security. But he will not do this to buy her love. Love cannot be bought. He will do it as the response of love to love. When a man responds to the love of God in Christ he gives up all confidence in himself and knows that his acceptance is based on the infinite mercy of God. But if his response to the love of God in Christ is genuine he must seek to live in a manner that is worthy of the destiny to which God has called him. Good works are not the basis of his acceptance; they are a proper expression of his response in love to the love of Christ for him.

The doctrine of salvation by faith is directed against all forms of work righteousness. Paul made it central in all of his preaching. He found in it God's answer to those who would require the Gentiles as a condition of salvation to receive circumcision and to keep the law of Moses. Paul and Peter were not Gentile sinners, but they had to learn that for them as for the Gentiles salvation came by faith alone. Luther rediscovered this doctrine and made it the basis of his whole attack on the system of penance which Rome had set up.

But while the doctrine of salvation by faith alone is directed to those of prestige and privilege, it is also directed to "Gentile sinners." It was the basis upon which Paul preached the gospel to all mankind. Wesley in his day rediscovered this doctrine, first in his personal experience and then in his preaching. It was the basis of his proclamation of the gospel to the great unchurched masses of his generation. And Booth found the same doctrine to be the heart of his preaching of the gospel to the human wreckage of the slums of our industrial society. To the man who is down and out, a message of salvation through the keeping of the law is not a message of hope. But the message of the grace of God and the offer of a salvation which is available for all who will receive it is good news to lost men. The forgiveness of God is not something we can merit. All that we can do is to be willing to receive it. God in Christ is reconciling the world unto himself. He has committed to his messengers the word of reconciliation. Paul writes: "We are ambassadors for Christ, God making his appeal through us. We beseech you on behalf of Christ, be reconciled to God" (2 Corinthians 5:20).

We must realize, of course, that the call of God is always a call to holiness. We must remember this when we preach to those who have sunk to the lowest depths of sin. Men are not saved so that they can continue in sin. The man whom God has justified must begin to live as a child of God. But the man who has accepted the salvation which God has wrought out in Jesus Christ will find that he is set in a new relation to God and that in this relation he will be able in the power of the Holy Spirit to begin to live the life of a child of God. Paul could write to the Corinthians: "Do you not know that the unrighteous will not inherit the kingdom of God? Do not be deceived; neither the immoral, nor idolaters, nor adulterers, nor homosexuals, nor thieves, nor the greedy, nor drunkards, nor revilers, nor robbers will inherit the kingdom of God. And such were some of you. But you were washed, you were sanctified, you were justified in the name of the Lord Jesus Christ and in the Spirit of our God" (1 Corinthians 6:9-11).

Paul could think through the membership of his church at Corinth and know that among them there were those who had been adulterers, or homosexuals, or thieves, or robbers, or drunkards. But these people had found salvation through putting their faith in what God had done for them in Christ. And in Christ they had found power for victorious living. The gospel of salvation by faith alone is the only gospel for lost and broken men.

# X

## THE FEAR OF THE LORD

*Scripture Background—2 Corinthians 5:6-15.*

"Knowing the fear of the Lord, we persuade men."—2 Corinthians 5:11.

The concept of the fear of the Lord is not popular today. Men have presented Jesus in terms of his love, his tenderness, his compassion. They have thought of him as a man of sorrows and acquainted with grief. They have pictured him as one so gentle that he would not crush a bruised reed or quench a dimly burning flax. They have seen him as the seeking Savior offering forgiveness to all who would come unto him. It comes to us therefore with something of a shock when Paul speaks of "Knowing the fear of the Lord."

But Paul speaks for the believing community of the New Testament when he says that Christians know the fear of the Lord. And he follows this concept to its logical conclusion when he says, "Knowing the fear of the Lord, we persuade men." The urgency of the New Testament proclamation is grounded in the knowledge of the fear of the Lord.

If we are to understand this concept we must see it in its setting in the fifth chapter of Second Corinthians. In the verses which precede our text Paul has described the Christian pilgrimage as a life in which men walk by faith without the visible presence of the Lord. He then goes on to say that for the Christian to be absent from the body is to be at home with the Lord. He expresses here the assured hope of Christians that when they have completed their life in this present world they will pass through death to a world in which they know the presence of the Lord in a manner which is not possible in our earthly life. Because he expects to come at death into a life in which he stands in the presence of the Lord, Paul seeks during his life in the body to live in a manner that will be pleasing to him.

It is in this setting that he makes the statement, "For we must all appear before the judgment seat of Christ, so that each one may receive good or evil, according to what he has done in the body" (2 Corinthians 5:10). While Paul up to this time has been thinking primarily of Christians in their experiences in this world and the next, it is evident that when he says "*we must all* appear before the judgment seat of Christ," he is thinking of all mankind. This is clear because he moves at once from this verse to the urgency of persuading men during the period of their earthly life to prepare for the time when they must appear before the judgment seat of Christ. It is evident also from the suggestion that some will receive good and some will receive evil. We need to be careful in our use of language here. When Paul says that some men may receive "evil" when they stand before the judgment seat of Christ, he would not for a moment suggest that the risen Lord would ever do that which is evil. The judgment is good news or bad news in terms of its meaning to the person who receives it. But it is a judgment which is just, and it is a judgment which is based on that which a man has done in the body. There is a sense in which the Lord makes manifest the decisions we have made.

When the first Christians spoke of the fear of the Lord, they were thinking of the One who is seated at the right hand of the Father and is the ultimate judge of every human being. They believed that every man at the end of his earthly life would have to stand before the judgment seat of Christ to receive of him good or evil, in accordance with his deeds done in the body. Because they knew this, they knew the fear of the Lord. But the figure of a risen Lord who is the ultimate judge of every human being is not a distortion of the church's memory of her Lord in the days of his flesh. We can properly speak of him as "gentle Jesus, meek and mild." But we must not do this to the exclusion of recognizing the sterner aspects of his character. To many of the people of his generation he was a man of offense. If there were some who loved him, there were others who hated him. And in the end those who hated him prevailed over those who loved him, and he was put to death. In the famous painting "Christ Before Pilate," by Munkacsy, there is in the forefront of the picture a big burly man who is holding a spear and is looking at Jesus. The artist has exhausted his skill in painting in this man's face hate and fury. If we ask who he hates, the answer is Jesus. Jesus himself was capable of wrath, and he could call forth the wrath of men.

Jesus said to the scribes and Pharisees: "You serpents, you brood of vipers, how are you to escape being sentenced to hell?" (Matthew 23:33). The phrase "sentenced to hell" shocks us, but these are the words of Jesus. Jesus has a profound sense of the impending judgment that is to come on Jerusalem. As he approaches the city in the triumphal entry, he weeps over Jerusalem. He weeps because he knows the certainty of judgment for the city which has failed to know the day of her visitation. And he bids the daughters of Jerusalem who follow him weeping to the cross to weep not for him but for themselves and for their children as they face the judgment that is to come (Luke 23:28).

Paul in his speech on Mars Hill points to the resurrection of Jesus as the assurance that God has given to all men of a day when he will judge the world through Christ. He says: "The times of ignorance God overlooked, but now he commands all men everywhere to repent, because he has fixed a day on which he will judge the world in righteousness by a man whom he has appointed, and of this he has given assurance to all men by raising him from the dead" (Acts 17:30-31). It is clear that the MAN whom God has appointed to judge the world is the man Christ Jesus.

Paul is undoubtedly aware of the capacity of Jesus for wrath in the days of his flesh and of the certainty of judgment for a civilization which persists in defying the laws of God. He knows that judgment is built into the structure of the moral order. But when he says, "Knowing the fear of the Lord, we persuade men," he is thinking specifically of that time when every man at the end of his earthly existence must stand before the judgment seat of Christ. Paul is certain that every human being must appear before the judgment seat of Christ. He is confident that every man must stand before the Lord to be judged according to what he has done in the body. As he bears witness to the reconciliation that God has wrought out in Christ, he pleads with men on behalf of Christ to be reconciled to God. He knows that men are responsible for whether or not they accept the salvation that God has made available to them in Christ. As the spokesman for Christ he beseeches men not to receive the grace of God in vain. He urges the necessity for an immediate decision as he says: "Behold, now is the acceptable time; behold, now is the day of salvation" (2 Corinthians 6:2).

Paul believes that every man who hears the proclamation of what God has done for him in Christ is immediately set in the place of decision. If he believes the message he has heard he must respond in repentance in which he turns from his sin unto God, in faith in which he acknowledges Jesus as Lord, and in new obedience in which he begins to live as a child of God. If he rejects the message he adds to his other sins the sin of not accepting God's offer of salvation in Christ. This is a decision which has to be made in the context of our earthly life. But it is also a decision that may be eternal in its consequences.

Paul does not attempt to spell out the judgment that men will receive from the Lord as they stand at his judgment seat. He leaves it with the statement that they will receive good or evil according to what they have done in the body. But Paul is quite confident that those who have accepted Jesus Christ as Lord and Savior while they are in the body will be acknowledged as his in the day of judgment. He writes to the Romans: "There is therefore now no condemnation for those who are in Christ Jesus" (Romans 8:1). He elaborates this as he writes: "If God is for us, who is against us? He who did not spare his own Son but gave him up for us all, will he not also give us all things with him? Who shall bring any charge against God's elect? It is God who justifies; who is to condemn? Is it Christ Jesus, who died, yes, who was raised from the dead, who is at the right hand of God, who indeed intercedes for us?" (Romans 8:31-34).

The fate of those who reject the offer of salvation which God has made in Christ is God's decision and not man's. Paul in one impassioned passage predicts the judgment that those who oppose the gospel will receive on Christ's return. In Second Thessalonians, Paul encourages the Thessalonians when they are suffering severe persecution as he writes to them: "God deems it just to repay with affliction those who afflict you, and to grant rest with us to you who are afflicted, when the Lord Jesus is revealed from heaven with his mighty angels in flaming fire, inflicting vengeance upon those who do not know God and upon those who do not obey the gospel of our Lord Jesus" (2 Thessalonians 1:6-8). It is interesting to observe here that Paul, who knows of "the love of Christ which surpasses knowledge" (Ephesians 3:19), does not seem to have any difficulty in combining his knowledge of the love of Christ with the picture of him as the one who administers the righteous judgment of God on those who obey not the gospel. Paul spells out this judgment as he says: "They shall suffer the punishment of eternal destruction and exclusion from the presence of the Lord and from the glory of his might, when he comes on that day to be glorified in his saints, and to be marveled at in all who have believed, because our testimony to you was believed" (2 Thessalonians 1:9-10). Paul does not define the phrase "eternal destruction." It could mean annihilation or it could mean eternal punishment. He does insist that part of the judgment which the wicked will receive will be exclusion "from the presence of the Lord and from the glory of his might." We will leave the details of this judgment to the Lord, in the confidence that his decisions will be just and right. We can be certain that all men must stand before the judgment seat of Christ, and that those who have received the reconciliation which he has wrought out will not be condemned and that those who have not believed the gospel will be punished.

It is because Paul knows the fear of the Lord that he knows also the urgency of seeking to persuade men to accept the salvation that is offered to them while they have the opportunity. Part of the decay of preaching in the modern world is the loss of this sense of urgency. When men encounter the proclamation of the gospel they are forced to make a decision for or against Christ which is eternal in its consequences. The urgency of Paul is rooted in his knowledge that the eternal destinies of men are involved in their response to the gospel.

F. W. H. Myers has caught this sense of urgency as he puts the following words in the mouth of Paul:

Oft when the word is on me to deliver
Lifts the illusion and the truth lies bare;
Desert or throng, the city or the river,
Melts in a lucid Paradise of air,—

Only like souls I see the folk thereunder,
Bound who should conquer, slaves who should be kings,—
Hearing their one hope with an empty wonder,
Sadly contented in a show of things;—

Then with a rush the intolerable craving
Shivers throughout me like a trumpet-call,—
Oh to save these! to perish for their saving,
Die for their life, be offered for them all![12]

In the urgency of preaching there are times when the external things should fade away as the preacher looks at his congregation. He ceases to see them as rich and poor, young and old, men and women. He sees them as souls, as human beings who must accept or reject God's offer in Christ. He knows that their eternal destinies are involved in this decision that they must make in the days of their being at home in the body. He knows that he is offering them their one hope. He seeks to persuade men with the urgency of the man who knows the fear of the Lord.

The urgency of a decision while there still is time is set forth by Jesus in the parable of the Wise and Foolish Virgins (Matthew 25:1-13). The point of the parable is that there was a time when the five foolish virgins could have made the necessary preparation so that they could be sure to be ready when the bridegroom came. But they did not make this preparation when they could, and after his coming it was too late. Tennyson has expressed the sheer tragedy of this as we think of human beings who could have been ready for their Lord at his coming but have waited until the day of opportunity is past. The poem is found as the song of the little maid in "Guinevere":

Late, late, so late! and dark the night and chill!
Late, late, so late! but we can enter still.
Too late, too late! Ye cannot enter now.

No light had we; for that we do repent,
And learning this, the bridegroom will relent.
Too late, too late! Ye cannot enter now.

No light! so late! and dark and chill the night!
O, let us in, that we may find the light!
Too late, too late! ye cannot enter now.

Have we not heard the bridegroom is so sweet?
O, let us in, tho' late, to kiss his feet!
No, no, too late! ye cannot enter now.[13]

Men cannot trifle with God's offer of salvation. Now is the accepted time. Now is the day of salvation. Tomorrow may be too late. "We are ambassadors for Christ, God making his appeal through us. We beseech you on behalf of Christ, be reconciled to God" (2 Corinthians 5:20).

# XI

## THE PROVIDENCE OF GOD

*Scripture Background—Romans 8:26-39.*

"And we know that all things work together for good to them that love God, to them who are the called according to his purpose."—Romans 8:28 (K.J.V.).

Dr. Frank Price, Sr., wrote a tract entitled "In Any Emergency, Dial Romans 8:28." It was his custom to carry copies of this tract with him and to leave them with those he visited in the hospitals. It was his conviction that we have here a great promise to which Christians can turn in time of need. In contrast there have been many sincere people who have felt that Paul overstated his case when he said that all things work together for good. They have felt that the observed facts of the world in which they live do not support the statement that things work together for good.

We should remember, of course, that Paul was not unacquainted with suffering and that he was not ignorant of the reality and power of evil in the world. In Second Corinthians, chapter 11, when as part of his argument he needs to call attention to his sufferings, he tells us that five times he has received of the Jews forty lashes less one, that three times he has been beaten with rods, that three times he has been shipwrecked, and that he has spent a night and a day adrift in the sea. The man who wrote the description of the pagan world in Romans 1:18-32 was not without some contact with evil. And the Christian community for which Paul speaks was not a secure and prosperous community. In the verses which immediately follow our text, he mentions tribulation, distress, persecution, famine, nakedness, peril, and the sword as among the experiences of the community with which he was identified. He describes the

church of his day in the words of the Forty-fourth Psalm, in which
the psalmist describes the suffering of the people of God as he
writes:

"For thy sake we are being killed all the day long;
we are regarded as sheep to be slaughtered" (Romans 8:36).

What does Paul mean when he says that all things work together
for good? If we look up Romans 8:28 in the different translations
we will be surprised at the variety of ways in which this verse is
translated. We have given as our text the familiar translation of the
King James Version. The Revised Standard Version reads: "We
know that in everything God works for good with those who love
him, who are called according to his purpose." The New English
Bible gives a strange twist to the translation. It goes back to the
preceding verse, which refers to the Holy Spirit, and translates:
"and in everything, as we know, he [the Spirit] co-operates for
good with those who love God and are called according to his purpose."

Why is there such diversity of translation—and of translations
which radically change the meaning? Part of the trouble is with the
question of the text. The word "God" as the subject of the sentence
is not in the text upon which the King James Version is based. It is
to be found, however, in a number of excellent manuscripts. The
Revised Standard Version is probably right in making God the
subject of the sentence. This has sound textual support, and it suits
the movement of the thought. A more important question is
whether the text says that in all things God works for good *with*
those who love him or that in all things God works for good *to* those
who love him. The latter translation is to be preferred as containing the substance of Paul's thought. Sanday and Headlam in their
great commentary on Romans translate it: "God worketh all things
for good to those who love him."[14]

It is true, of course, that in all things God works for good *with*
those who love him. When an idea is not contained in a particular
text, we are not to conclude that it is not true. God is good, and he
is ceaselessly working for good. Those who love God and seek to
work for good in their world do not stand alone. God is working

with and through them to accomplish his good purposes. God is working in ways that they know, and in ways that they do not know, to bring about the victory of good over evil.

But Paul in this text is affirming that God in all things is working for good to those who love him. When we say this we do not mean that God is not seeking the good of those who have failed to respond to his love. The miracle of God's love is that he loved us when we were hostile to him. But when men are in rebellion against God it may be necessary for God to let them reap the consequences of their sowing to the flesh. He may need to bring them to the end of their road in order that they may turn to him. The fate of those who do not love God is not being considered in this text.

When Paul says we know that in all things God is working for good to those who love him, he is not speaking in uncertain terms. He is disclosing the knowledge of God that is at the heart of the Christian community. Tennyson in his *In Memoriam* writes:

> I held it truth, with him who sings
>   To one clear harp in divers tones,
>   That men may rise on stepping-stones
> Of their dead selves to higher things.
>
> But who shall so forecast the years
>   And find in loss a gain to match?
>   Or reach a hand thro' time to catch
> The far-off interest of tears?[15]

But Paul is not speaking uncertainly of "the far-off interest of tears." He is affirming with glad assurance his confidence that in all things God is working for good to them that love him.

Paul's confidence that God is working for good to those who love him is grounded in his belief in the sovereignty of God. In the verses which follow, we see the purpose of God as he chooses and calls individuals and plans that they shall be conformed to the image of his Son, that he (the Christ) might be the first-born among many brethren. God is with those who have responded to his call. He justifies them; that is, he accepts them as righteous in his sight, and calls them to become his children. Those whom God has called he sanctifies. This is not stated in the verses before us. It is stated in 1 Corinthians 1:30 and is integral to the thought of Paul. God is at work with those he has called as he enables them more and more to die unto sin and to live unto righteousness. Those whom God has called he glorifies. This refers to the time when freed from sin we take our place in the eternal kingdom of God.

In this passage the emphasis is on the divine sovereignty. We are not to think that this is emphasized to the destruction of human freedom. Sanday and Headlam comment: "There can be no question that St. Paul fully recognizes the freedom of the human will. The large part which exhortation plays in his letters is conclusive proof of this. But whatever the extent of human freedom there must be behind it the Divine Sovereignty."[16] Paul could include both human freedom and the divine activity in human life as he wrote to the Philippians: "Work out your own salvation with fear and trembling; for God is at work in you, both to will and to work for his good pleasure" (Philippians 2:12-13). It is God who sets the pattern of our lives, but we ourselves have a part in determining the way in which we respond to the things that God sends upon us.

When Paul says we know that in all things God works for good to those who love him, he is thinking of the word "good" in terms of the accomplishment of the purpose of God for those whom he has called. It is God's purpose that those whom he has called may "be conformed to the image of his Son, in order that he might be the first-born among many brethren." If we understand the word "good" in this sense we can begin to see the movement of the text. God is at work in the lives of his people in the process of molding them into the image of his Son. God is concerned not so much for our comfort as for our growth in holiness. If we are to be molded into the image of the Christ we must come to know the meaning of love for the unlovely, of compassion for the fallen, and of unwavering hostility to evil. A headmaster of a school for boys cannot always be concerned to keep the boys happy. He is not in the business of making boys happy. He has the much more serious task of making men out of boys.

Paul is keenly conscious of the suffering of the people of God. But he is also confident that when this suffering is looked at in the light of the glory that will finally be revealed in them, it will be seen in a deeper dimension and will be recognized as an expression of the love of God. In the eighteenth verse of the chapter in which our text is found, Paul writes: "I consider that the sufferings of this present time are not worth comparing with the glory that is to be revealed to us." In 2 Corinthians 4:17, he writes: "This slight momentary affliction is preparing for us an eternal weight of glory beyond all comparison."

While we cannot fully solve the mystery of the suffering of the righteous, we can see even in this world something of the meaning of a world of struggle, suffering, and sorrow. This is expressed in the poem "Lord, Take Away Pain." It was found written on the walls of a Denver hospital.

> The cry of man's anguish went up unto God,
> "Lord, take away pain!
> The shadow that darkens the world Thou hast made;
> The close-coiling chain
> That strangles the heart; the burden that weighs on the
> wings that would soar—
> Lord, take away pain from the world Thou hast made,
> That it love Thee the more!"
>
> Then answered the Lord to the cry of His world:
> "Shall I take away pain,
> And with it the power of the soul to endure,
> Made strong by the strain?
> Shall I take away pity, that knits heart to heart,
> And sacrifice high?
> Will ye lose all your heroes that lift from the fire
> White brows to the sky?
> Shall I take away love, that redeems with a price,
> And smiles at its loss?
> Can ye spare from your lives that would climb unto mine
> The Christ on His cross?"[17]

In the revelation of God which we have at the heart of the believing community of the New Testament, we do not have a theoretical solution to the problem of suffering. We do have as the revelation of God the figure of a suffering and dying Messiah. We are pointed to the God who suffers too. In the Christian community there is the knowledge of the God who "did not spare his own Son but gave him up for us all" (Romans 8:32). In the Christian revelation a suffering God stands by the side of a suffering man and suffers with and for him. We cannot impugn the God who suffers too.

The word "curriculum" in its root meaning stands for a course to be run. If we believe with Paul in the sovereignty of God we know that the things which life brings us come as part of the purpose of God for us. It is God who sets for us the course we must run. As he sets this course he is concerned to accomplish his purpose for us—his plan that we shall be molded into the moral and spiritual likeness of the Christ. He sets the pattern of our lives that through this discipline we may become partakers of his holiness. We must meet the experiences that life brings us in the hope that we may so react to them that the purpose of God in sending them will be accomplished in us. It is here that the divine sovereignty emerges as a word of grace and comfort. We know that the God who has called us and planned for us to be conformed to the image of his Son is able to accomplish his purpose in us. Paul ends his first letter to the Thessalonians with the prayer, "May the God of peace himself sanctify you wholly; and may your spirit and soul and body be kept sound and blameless at the coming of our Lord Jesus Christ. *He who calls you is faithful, and he will do it*" (1 Thessalonians 5:23-24). The God who has come to us in Jesus Christ is the God who "worketh all things for good to those who love him, to those who are the called according to his purpose." The New Testament points us to the God who is able to keep us from falling and to present us "without blemish before the presence of his glory with rejoicing" (Jude 24).

# XII

## THE LOVE OF GOD IN CHRIST JESUS OUR LORD

*Scripture Background—Romans 8:28-39.*

"I am sure that neither death, nor life, nor angels, nor principalities, nor things present, nor things to come, nor powers, nor height, nor depth, nor anything else in all creation, will be able to separate us from the love of God in Christ Jesus our Lord."—Romans 8:38-39.

It is reported that a traveler once stood in the presence of the great Sphinx of Egypt and said, "O Sphinx, if I could ask you one question it would be, 'Is the universe friendly?'" The question would not be easily answered in terms of our knowledge of the natural world. We have made amazing progress in our understanding of the structure of the physical universe. Through such sciences as chemistry, biology, geology, and physics we have entered into an understanding of the world around us which was quite unknown to the ancient world. We know the secret of atomic energy, and we are seriously talking in terms of an expedition to the moon. With our advancing knowledge we have been able to harness the energies of the world of nature and put them to the service of man.

Our knowledge of the world around us reveals a world of law and order, a world of cause and effect. It reveals a dependable world rather than a world of caprice. But it reveals also a world that seems to be devoid of moral purpose or of concern for human welfare. Is man involved in a world of nature that is completely indifferent to his fate? Can we believe that at the heart of the universe there is a personal God who knows us and loves us? Can it be that the Lord of the universe cares for me? Tennyson phrased our question when in his poem "Vastness" he turns from his sorrow at the death of his friend to ask: "What is it all but a trouble of ants in the gleam of a million million of suns?"[18]

Robert Browning in "Cleon" states the dilemma of both ancient and modern man in his search for God. Cleon is a Greek poet and artist, a contemporary of the Apostle Paul, who is writing in reply to a letter from King Protus. The king has congratulated him on the immortality he will attain through his works. The king in contrast feels that he is leaving nothing memorable or enduring. But Cleon is not satisfied with immortality through what he has accomplished. He writes with dread of the end of his life, when

> "I, I the feeling, thinking, acting man,
> The man who loved his life so over-much,
> Sleep in my urn. It is so horrible,
> I dare at times imagine to my need
> Some future state revealed to us by Zeus,
> Unlimited in capability
> For joy, as this is in desire for joy,
> —To seek which, . . .
> Freed by the throbbing impulse we call death,
> We burst there as the worm into the fly,
> Who, while a worm still, wants his wings. But no!
> Zeus has not yet revealed it; and alas,
> He must have done so, were it possible!

"He is sorry he cannot tell the king where he can send a message to 'one called Paulus'. He had heard of him and indeed some disciples of his [Paul's] had landed at his island and

> "preached him and Christ;
> And (as I gathered from a bystander)
> The doctrine could be held by no sane man.
> .   .   .   .   .   .   .
> Thou wrongest our philosophy, O king,
> In stooping to inquire of such an one . . ."

To Cleon, "It is obviously inconceivable that Paul could have access to any secret knowledge not available to the culture of Greece."[19]

But Paul and the Christian community of the New Testament would have disagreed with Cleon. They could have cried out, "We know the love of God which is in Christ Jesus our Lord." And because they had this knowledge they had some great affirmations to make about the significance of man's life on earth. They knew that the message they were proclaiming was foolishness to the Greeks. But they were convinced also that it was in agreement with reality. They found the consummation of their knowledge of the love of God in his self-disclosure in Jesus Christ. But they knew that they stood also in the heritage of the people of God of the Old Testament.

The central theme of the Old Testament is its witness to the way in which God has taken the initiative and made himself known to man. The writer of the 103rd Psalm says of the Lord:

"He made known his ways to Moses,
  his acts to the people of Israel."

He then goes on to say:

"The LORD is merciful and gracious,
  slow to anger and abounding in steadfast love.

. . . . . . .

". . . the steadfast love of the LORD is from everlasting to
    everlasting
  upon those who fear him,
  and his righteousness to children's children,
to those who keep his covenant
  and remember to do his commandments."[20]

The writers of the New Testament knew the story of the mighty acts of God in the history of Israel. They knew also the love of God in Jesus Christ our Lord. Paul writes: "It is the God who said, 'Let light shine out of darkness,' who has shone in our hearts to give the light of the knowledge of the glory of God in the face of Christ" (2 Corinthians 4:6).

Philip voices the yearning of man for a knowledge of God when he says to Jesus, "Lord, show us the Father, and we shall be satisfied." And Jesus replies to him, "Have I been with you so long, and yet you do not know me, Philip? He who has seen me has seen the Father" (John 14:8-9). When the first Christians came to the conviction that Jesus was the Son of God, they came also to the understanding that the attitudes of Jesus were a revelation of the heart of God. Paul in Romans 8:37 refers to Jesus as "him who loved us." In Ephesians Paul prays that his readers may know the love of Christ which surpasses knowledge (Ephesians 3:19). The followers of Jesus were sure that in their knowledge of the love of Jesus they had come also to the knowledge of the love of God.

The New Testament writers found the final revelation of the love of God in his readiness to send his Son to die for sinning man. Paul writes: "God shows his love for us in that while we were yet sinners Christ died for us" (Romans 5:8). John writes: "In this is love, not that we loved God but that he loved us and sent his Son to be the expiation for our sins" (1 John 4:10). Consider also in this connection the familiar John 3:16: "God so loved the world that he gave his only Son, that whoever believes in him should not perish but have eternal life."

The love of God which is made known in Jesus Christ our Lord is a seeking love. Jesus speaks of the joy in heaven over one sinner who repents. When he wants to depict the seeking love of God he describes a woman who searches diligently for one lost coin and rejoices when she finds it. He pictures a shepherd who leaves the ninety and nine sheep safe in the fold and goes out and searches for the one lost sheep until he finds it. He describes the Father who waits for the prodigal son to return and runs to meet him, rejoicing in the return of his son (Luke 15). In fact, the whole story of Jesus is the story of the God who is for us. It is the story of the God who "did not spare his own Son but gave him up for us all" (Romans 8:32). In his *Church Dogmatics,* Karl Barth entitles his section on redemption, "The Journey of the Son into the Far Country." The New Testament narrative points us to the God who at great cost to himself is seeking man by the way of the cross.

The love of God which is in Jesus Christ our Lord is a holy love. God loves us, and because he loves us he wants us to be worthy of his love. The love of God is the love of a Being who is eternally hostile to sin. In the death of his Son he makes the expiation for our sins. And his call to us is always the call to repent of sin and accept his forgiveness, turning from sin "with full purpose of, and endeavor after, new obedience."[21] His purpose for us is that we may be "conformed to the image of his Son, that he might be the first-born among many brethren" (Romans 8:29).

Because God is love he is irrevocably involved in the struggle with evil. He restrains evil in his justice, but in his love he seeks to overcome evil and to bring the sinner to loving response to his love. Hugh Martin in summing up the faith of Robert Browning writes: "To hold firmly on the one hand to the reality of the moral struggle, and on the other hand to the ultimate victory of the good, to the independence of the human soul and to the overruling Providence of God, is no easy faith; but Browning will not compromise on either hand. For him, love is God's last but sufficient word."[22]

The love of God which is in Christ Jesus our Lord is a jealous love. The God who comes to us here is the God who demands our complete devotion. He does not permit us to have other gods before him. We can see this kind of love in the marriage relation. The love of the husband should be a jealous love. His love is not a holy love if he is indifferent to whether or not his wife is faithful to him. The love of God which has come to us in Jesus Christ our Lord is a love which calls for our full surrender.

In the passage before us, the reference to the love of God in Christ Jesus our Lord is part of a larger statement in which Paul affirms his conviction that nothing will ever be able to come between the believer and the love of God which has come to him in Jesus Christ. The full statement is: "I am sure that neither death, nor life, nor angels, nor principalities, nor things present, nor things to come, nor powers, nor height, nor depth, nor anything else in all creation, will be able to separate us from the love of God in Christ Jesus our Lord" (Romans 8:38-39). Paul exhausts language to say that nothing in God's universe can come between him and those whom he has claimed as his own in Jesus Christ. This is not the faith of a people who are living in comfort and in ease. This is the faith of a persecuted minority who are being called upon to suffer for their faith.

In the midst of their distress the Christians know that they have been laid hold of by a love that will prevail. Paul can say, "In all these things we are more than conquerors through him who loved us" (Romans 8:37). The Christians can face the future unafraid because they know that if God is for them no one can be successfully against them. They can cry out, "He who did not spare his own Son but gave him up for us all, will he not also give us all things with him?" (Romans 8:32). In particular they are able to affirm their faith that death will not be able to separate them from the love of God which is in Jesus Christ their Lord. Because they know the love of God which is in Christ Jesus, Christians can sing as the word of God to the believer:

> The soul that on Jesus hath leaned for repose,
> I will not, I will not desert to his foes;
> That soul, though all hell should endeavor to shake,
> I'll never, no, never, no, never forsake.[23]

# XIII

## THE HOPE OF ETERNAL LIFE

*Scripture Background—2 Corinthians 4:16—5:5.*

"We know that if the earthly tent we live in is destroyed, we have a building from God, a house not made with hands, eternal in the heavens."—2 Corinthians 5:1.

In this verse, Paul says that for the Christian the dissolution of the body means not annihilation but translation to a higher state of existence. He does not argue for his position here. He simply affirms it as knowledge that is found at the heart of the Christian community. The contrasts of the text are noticeable. The earthly body is compared to a tent. It is contrasted with a building erected by God. The earthly body is temporal, the house not made with hands is eternal. The body which we know now is a thing of earth. The body for which we wait is in heaven. Paul makes here no effort to describe the nature of the house not made with hands. It is part of that which God has prepared for those who love him. Paul is confident that for the Christian, life is not moving toward annihilation, or something worse than annihilation, but toward an experience in which mortality is swallowed up by life.

Paul makes this affirmation against the background of his realization that all human life is marked by existence unto death. In the sixteenth verse of the fourth chapter he has written: "We do not lose heart. Though our outer nature is wasting away, our inner nature is being renewed every day." When Paul wrote Second Corinthians he had just passed through an experience in which for a time he despaired of life itself (2 Corinthians 1:8-11). As he writes the fourth chapter, he does not expect to live until Christ's return, but he does express the hope that Christ will raise him up so that he will stand along with his Corinthian converts in the presence of his Lord (2 Corinthians 4:14). He writes with a profound sense of the temporal nature of the things which are seen and the certainty that it is the things which are not seen that are eternal.

It is not merely the fact of death that disturbs us. We face the inevitable fact of aging. The little child grows stronger every day, but there comes a time in every life when the process of aging sets in. In most cases, the man of fifty does not retain the physical vitality which he knew at twenty-five. And if people live long enough they move inevitably toward the breakdown of both physical and mental powers. The body which we can see and touch belongs to the things that are transient. But in the midst of his realization that his outer nature is wasting away, Paul affirms the certainty of the existence of a building from God, a house not made with hands, eternal in the heavens.

What are the grounds of this hope which the apostle so confidently affirms? We can be sure that Paul's certainty of the existence of the house not made with hands grew out of his encounter with Jesus Christ. The hope of the resurrection of the dead did not begin with Jesus. In the Judaism of Paul's day, it was a hope that was central to the faith of the Pharisees. This hope was not shared by the Sadducees. Some years after the writing of the letter to the Corinthians, Paul was able to break up a meeting of the Sanhedrin by setting the Sadducees against the Pharisees as he insisted that he was on trial for the hope of the resurrection of the dead (Acts 23:6-10). Jesus did not originate the hope of the resurrection, but he reaffirmed it and tied it to himself (John 5:19-29). When Jesus stands before Martha as she weeps for her dead brother, he says: "I am the resurrection and the life; he who believes in me, though he die, yet shall he live, and whoever lives and believes in me shall never die" (John 11:25-26). In this case he confirms the claim he has made by the raising of Lazarus as the sign that he is indeed the One who has been sent by the Father (John 11:42).

In the debate with the Sadducees during the passion week, Jesus clearly repudiates the position of the Sadducees and insists that when God reveals himself to Moses as the God of Abraham it means that Abraham is alive with God. In this setting he says: "The sons of this age marry and are given in marriage; but those who are accounted worthy to attain to that age and to the resurrection from the dead neither marry nor are given in marriage, for they cannot die any more, because they are equal to angels and are sons of God, being sons of the resurrection" (Luke 20:34-36). It is clear that in this passage Jesus speaks with confidence of a resurrection world of God. He refers also to those who are accounted worthy to attain to the resurrection from the dead. We can be certain that Jesus points to a world beyond death, to a world in which at least some people have attained to the state in which they "cannot die any more."

In the familiar fourteenth chapter of John, Jesus says to his disciples: "In my Father's house are many rooms; if it were not so, would I have told you that I go to prepare a place for you? And when I go and prepare a place for you, I will come again and will take you to myself, that where I am you may be also" (John 14: 2-3).

Apart from the witness to his resurrection, Jesus would have stood as one of the great teachers of mankind who held firmly to the hope of the life beyond the grave. But it was the resurrection of Jesus that made this hope a burning reality in the lives of his followers. Peter writes: "Blessed be the God and Father of our Lord Jesus Christ! By his great mercy we have been born anew to a living hope through the resurrection of Jesus Christ from the dead, and to an inheritance which is imperishable, undefiled, and unfading, kept in heaven for you" (1 Peter 1:3-4).

Many of the first Christians had seen the risen Lord. Paul was not among the original witnesses, but he had the experience of encounter with the risen Christ as he was on his way to Damascus. Paul joins the company of those who were chosen by God to be witnesses to the resurrection of Jesus. These first Christians could not realize the full significance of the thing they had seen. But they knew with certainty that there was a resurrection world of God that lies beyond death.

It was the belief that for them death was not annihilation but translation to a higher state of existence that nerved the first Christians to be faithful unto death in their witness to Jesus as Lord. They could express their faith as they sang:

"If we have died with him, we shall also live with him;

if we endure, we shall also reign with him" (2 Timothy
2:11-12).

This was the testimony of the aged Polycarp as he faced death by
burning with the prayer, "O Lord God Almighty . . . I bless Thee
in that Thou hast deemed me worthy of this day and hour; that I
may take a portion among the martyrs in the cup of Christ, to the
resurrection of eternal life of both soul and body."[24]

In the verses that follow our text Paul finds himself in a strange
dilemma. He knows that when he is present in the body he is in a
sense absent from the Lord. He knows that it is only in the life
beyond death that he comes into the full meaning of being present
with the Lord. He faces a dilemma similar to that which he knows
when writing to the Philippians, "For to me to live is Christ, and
to die is gain. If it is to be life in the flesh, that means fruitful labor
for me. Yet which I shall choose I cannot tell. I am hard pressed between the two. My desire is to depart and be with Christ, for that
is far better. But to remain in the flesh is more necessary on your
account" (Philippians 1:21-24). Paul does not seek death, but he
does yearn for the time when mortality will be swallowed up by
life. This yearning becomes particularly strong in times of sickness
when he realizes afresh the way in which the body that he now
knows is wasting away. The deep yearning of Christians for the
final experience of entering the heavenly home is one of the marks
of the Christian life and one of the things that point to the reality
of the house not made with hands, in the heavens.

Paul goes on to say that the God who has prepared us for the
experience of entering the heavenly home has given us the Spirit as
a guarantee. It is the Spirit that brings home to us the truth of the
great affirmation concerning the home in the heavens. Paul writes:
"When we cry, 'Abba! Father!' it is the Spirit himself bearing witness with our spirit that we are children of God, and if children,
then heirs, *heirs of God* and *fellow heirs with Christ,* provided we
suffer with him in order that *we may also be glorified with him*"
(Romans 8:15-17).

We know that the belief in the existence of the house not made
with hands, eternal in the heavens, was part of the faith of Paul and
of the believing community of the New Testament. Can we affirm

this faith with equal confidence in the midst of the secularism and the atheism of much of the modern world? The thought forms of Paul and his world are not ours. Paul lived in a world that believed in a three-storied universe, with the earth in the center and heaven above and hell beneath. We do not live in this world. We know the vast reaches of space. We are conscious of stages of life on the earth that cover many millions of years. But the central core of the Christian message is not affected by our changing thought forms. Christ came to call men in this world to an eternal inheritance. The salvation which he brought was a salvation that penetrated death.

And with all of the changing patterns of man's life on earth he still faces the inevitable breakdown of his body and the certainty of death. Rev. W. I. Howell, Jr., who ministered in the camps around Hamlet, North Carolina, during the Second World War, tells the story of a boy who came to him and asked for a conference. The boy said that he had been brought up in a nominally Christian home but that he had never taken seriously the matter of his attitude to religion. He went on to say that his experiences in the camp had forced him to realize his need of a faith to live by. He knew now that he needed a faith that would give him guidance in life's decisions and strength for the demands that life was making on him. After saying that he needed a faith to live by, the boy was quiet for a few minutes and then he went on: "Mr. Howell, our unit has been issued equipment which means that we are being sent to the South Pacific. This means that some of us will not be coming back. Mr. Howell, I need a faith to die by." Christianity is a faith to live by. It calls men to holiness and purity and love. It issues in a life of ministry to man in the service of God. But Christianity is also a faith to die by. It holds out to the believer the hope of a complete redemption in which he will find that beyond the dissolution of the earthly body there is waiting for him a dwelling place of God, a house not made with hands, eternal in the heavens. It points him to the inheritance which is imperishable, undefiled, and unfading which is kept in heaven for him. We know that we cannot give a positive description of the heavenly home, but we know that for the believer death is not annihilation but translation to a higher state of existence. We know also that it is an experience in which the believer passes into the realized presence of his Lord.

# XIV

## THE CONSUMMATION

*Scripture Background—1 Corinthians 15:35-58; 1 Thessalonians 4:13-18; Philippians 3:20-21; Colossians 3:1-4.*

"Our commonwealth is in heaven, and from it we await a Savior, the Lord Jesus Christ, who will change our lowly body to be like his glorious body, by the power which enables him even to subject all things to himself."—Philippians 3:20-21.

Is there a far-off divine event toward which the whole creation moves? Is man on our planet moving toward annihilation or toward a divine consummation? Will the Christ who has come come again? Will he come this time in glory and in power? These and similar questions are not irrelevant to a world that must live with the threat of thermonuclear destruction. Is there a word of hope for a world in which it is possible to let loose within a few minutes enough explosive power to destroy a large percentage of the human race and to render great areas of the earth uninhabitable?

The church of the New Testament expected the end of the present world order and the return of the Christ in the near future. The letters to the Thessalonians are dominated by the thought that the coming of the Christ is not far away. There are references to the coming of the Lord in every chapter of First Thessalonians. Paul hoped to be among those who were alive when the Christ came back. In First Thessalonians he writes: "We who are alive, who are left, shall be caught up together with them [the dead in Christ who have been raised] in the clouds to meet the Lord in the air" (1 Thessalonians 4:17). In 1 Corinthians 15, as he describes the return he writes: "We shall not all sleep, but we shall all be changed" (verse 51). These verses show that Paul was confident that some of those to whom he was writing would still be living when the Lord returned. Dr. Eugene C. Caldwell used to say to his classes that the New Testament was the literature of an intense catastrophic eschatological expectation. By this he meant that the New Testament was written in the expectancy of a sudden return of the Christ which would bring to an end the present world order and be the beginning of the establishment of the kingdom of God. The New Testament church was the community of those who were looking for the Savior from heaven.

When we realize the extent to which the preaching of the New Testament church was dominated by the expectancy of the return of the Christ, we are bound to ask why the fact that the Christ did not come as expected did not discredit the New Testament proclamation. How did the Christian community survive the delay in the return of the Lord? As we seek to answer this question, we should realize that Paul and the apostles never committed themselves to the setting of an actual date for the return of the Lord. They lived in the expectancy of an imminent return, but if pressed they would have admitted freely that they did not know the exact date of the Lord's coming. Even in the letters to the church at Thessalonica, Paul was consistently in conflict with some of the Thessalonians who felt that the coming of the Lord was so near that there was no need to work or to save for the future. Paul insists that the coming of the Lord will be like the coming of a thief in the night. The one thing that is certain about the coming of the thief is that he will plan to come when he is not expected. The first Christians hoped that the coming of the Lord would not be delayed, but we have in the church from the beginning the realization that the time of the coming was not known. In the Gospel of Mark, Jesus refers to the coming of the Son of Man as he says: "But of that day or that hour no one knows, not even the angels in heaven, nor the Son, but only the Father" (Mark 13:32). The first Christians waited for the coming of the Savior and they hoped it would be soon, but they knew that they did not know the time of the return.

While the New Testament Christians lived in the expectancy of the return, the real tension of their lives was between the resur-

rection world of God, which had been made known to them in the
resurrection of the Christ, and the visible world in which at present
they were living. The resurrection of Christ was more than a re-
suscitation in which life returned for a time to a dead body to enable
a person to live for a few more years in this present world order.
Jesus Christ passed through death. He presented himself alive to
his disciples after his Passion. He wrought in them the certainty
that he was alive. He appeared in a resurrection body that had
continuity with the body he had had in the days of his flesh. But
it was a resurrection body. Through their contact with the risen
Christ, the first Christians were given assured knowledge of the
existence of the resurrection world of God which lies beyond death.
The roots of their lives as Christians were in this resurrection
world. This is what Paul means when he says, "Our commonwealth
is in heaven." He expresses the same idea when he writes to the
Colossians: "If then you have been raised with Christ, seek the
things that are above, where Christ is, seated at the right hand of
God. Set your minds on things that are above, not on things
that are on earth. For you have died, and your life is hid with
Christ in God. When Christ who is our life appears, then you also
will appear with him in glory" (Colossians 3:1-4). Paul points to
the contrast between this world and the world to come when he
says: "We look not to the things that are seen but to the things
that are unseen; for the things that are seen are transient, but the
things that are unseen are eternal" (2 Corinthians 4:18). The first
Christians were strangers and pilgrims on the earth because they
had been made aware of the reality of another world. They knew
that the visible world was temporal and the resurrection world of
God was eternal. This was the abiding tension of their lives. It is
a tension that should mark the lives of Christians today.

The first Christians believed that the death of the individual involved for that individual a time of encounter in which he passed
from this visible world into the invisible world of God. They believed that every man would be made manifest before the judgment
seat of Christ (2 Corinthians 5:10). They believed that for the
Christian to be absent from the body was to be at home with the
Lord (2 Corinthians 5:8). No man knows exactly when death will

come to him. But every man knows that he must die. In the certainty of death and the uncertainty of the time of death we have for each individual a tension not essentially different from the tension of the first Christians, who waited for the coming of the Lord but did not know just when he would come.

Paul took his stand with the Christians who knew that their citizenship was in heaven and looked for the Savior from heaven. What did these Christians look for? We may oversimplify the matter, but we are not far wrong when we say that what they expected was the full disclosure of the resurrection world of God in which their life was already grounded. In describing the second coming, Paul uses the symbolism of Jewish eschatology. He speaks of a coming in the clouds, of a meeting with the Lord in the air, of the sounding of a trumpet, of the archangel's call, and so on. In particular he deals with spatial terms. Heaven is above. Earth is below. But no one knew better than Paul that he was dealing in symbolism. He was using the thought forms of his time to give an inadequate description of that which cannot be fully described.

But there are certain essential elements in this picture which can in part be stated. Paul believed that the coming of the Christ would be accompanied by whatever change was necessary in the created universe to make it a suitable environment for the new world that was being disclosed. We can think of this in terms of being delivered from the bondage of corruption into the glorious liberty of the children of God (Romans 8:21). We may think of this as the author of Second Peter does, in terms of a passing away of heaven and earth. If we do this we must always remember the words, "According to his promise we wait for new heavens and a new earth in which righteousness dwells" (2 Peter 3:13).

But the center of interest is not in the created universe but in people. Paul was confident that Christians who lived to the time of the return of the Lord would experience a change, a radical change which would fit them for life in the new world which was being disclosed. This is clearly stated in our text. Paul says, "We await a Savior . . . who will change our lowly body to be like his glorious body." There is no disparagement of the body in the Greek word that is translated "lowly." It is the body of earth. It is the only body that is suited to life in the world we know. Paul did expect a transformation of this body in which it would be made like unto the glorious body in which the risen Lord had manifested himself alive. In Philippians he states the necessity for this change. But in the latter part of the fifteenth chapter of First Corinthians he describes it in exalted and impassioned language.

The New Testament writers were confident that those who had fallen asleep in Christ would participate in the glory of the messianic reign along with those who were alive at his return. In 1 Thessalonians 4:15, Paul tells the Thessalonians that he has had a word of the Lord which assured him that the dead in Christ and those who are Christ's at his coming will share alike in the salvation which the Christ brings. In 1 Corinthians 15:52, he writes: "The trumpet will sound, and the dead will be raised *imperishable*." We cannot know just what this involves for the Christian dead because we do not know the condition in which they now exist. We do know that they will be raised *incorruptible*. They will share in the freedom from corruption which is the mark of the resurrection world of God.

Paul does not deal in detail with the fate of those who are not "Christ's at his coming" (1 Corinthians 15:23, K.J.V.). We do know that he felt a tremendous urgency to lead men to accept the gospel in their day of opportunity. In 2 Thessalonians 1:9, he says that those who do not obey the gospel "shall suffer the punishment of eternal destruction and exclusion from the presence of the Lord and from the glory of his might." In the thought of the New Testament it is a very serious matter for a man to come to death without being prepared to stand before the judgment seat of Christ, or for him to be found unprepared when the Lord comes to bring to an end the present world order and to give the full disclosure of the resurrection world of God. In the same letter from which our text is drawn, Paul expresses the hope that the time may come "that at the name of Jesus every knee should bow, in heaven and on earth and under the earth, and every tongue confess that Jesus Christ is Lord, to the glory of God the Father" (Philippians 2:10-11). But the expression of this hope does not diminish the urgency with which he would persuade men to accept the reconciliation which

God has made in Christ while the offer of salvation is still open to them.

We have been describing a radical transformation of the created universe, a change in the lives of those living in which the mortal puts on immortality, and a raising of the dead incorruptible. These are things that require a power that is quite unknown to us. But Paul says that Jesus Christ will be able to accomplish them "by the power which enables him even to subject all things to himself." Paul deals with this same subject in 1 Corinthians 15:24-28. He seems to say that God has committed to the Christ the power necessary to bring all things into subjection to him. We are dealing here with the power of the God who brought all things into being by the word of his power, with the power of the God who brought again from the dead the Lord Jesus Christ through the blood of the everlasting covenant, with the power of the God who seeks through Christ to reconcile the world unto himself. There has been committed to the Christ power that is adequate for the work he is to do.

In commenting on the power of the Christ to subject all things unto himself, Parry writes: "The subjection . . . spoken of cannot be limited to a mere mechanical or forcible beating down of alien things, but must signify what can alone be described as a true submission in the case of personal powers, expressed more fully by the *reconciling* of 2 Corinthians 5:18."[25] As we understand the concern of the Christ for a reconciliation that involves loving obedience, we can see the full nature of the task that has been committed unto him.

The ideas we have been discussing seem foreign to the life of the modern world. We live in a world of atomic energy and space exploration. We know a world the vastness of which would have been inconceivable to a man of the first century. We do not believe in the three-storied universe that was assumed in the time of Paul. We are not at home in the symbolism of Jewish eschatology. But the basic ideas which Paul sought to express in the thought forms of his day can be of vital significance to us. The Christian today must face death as one who waits for the Savior. If he is to find his way from the world he knows to the world that lies beyond death it must be with the help of the One who has said: "In my Father's house are many rooms; if it were not so, would I have told you that I go to prepare a place for you? And when I go and prepare a place for you, I will come again and will take you to myself, that where I am you may be also" (John 14:2-3). Modern man is as helpless as the man of the first century when he seeks to find his way to the resurrection world of God.

The modern world lives in the possibility of an atomic destruction that would dwarf all the terrors that up to this time have been seen on our earth. The human race has now the power to destroy itself and to render the earth uninhabitable for human beings. In the midst of these tensions it is well to hear again the testimony of the New Testament Christians as they wait for the Savior from heaven, the Lord Jesus Christ. They were confident that there had been committed to him the power of destroying every rule and every authority and power. They were confident that in time he would accomplish his purpose. They believed that history was moving not toward annihilation but toward the realization of the purpose of God in the creation of man. They would speak a strong word of hope to those who must live under the threat of thermonuclear destruction.

# XV

## THE CONTINUING VISION

*Scripture Background—2 Corinthians 5:11-21.*

"Wherefore we henceforth know no man after the flesh: even though we have known Christ after the flesh, yet now we know him so no more."—2 Corinthians 5:16 (A.S.V.).

What did Paul mean when he said, "We . . . know no man after the flesh"? The background of his statement is his understanding of the significance of the death of Christ. He is convinced that in the death of Christ "one has died for all." He draws from this the conclusion, "therefore all have died." By this he means that for every man a death has taken place which is accepted as if he had actually died for his sin. Because of this death God is ready to treat him as if the penalty for his sins had been paid in full. Paul goes on to say that Christ "died for all, that those who live might live no longer for themselves but for him who for their sake died and was raised." The purpose of the death of Christ is accomplished when those for whom he died cease to live for themselves and begin to live for the Christ who for their sake died and rose again.

When Paul came into contact with a person, he saw him, of course, "after the flesh." He became aware of the person's sex, of his approximate age, and of his race, whether Jew or Gentile, barbarian or Scythian. He made discriminating judgments concerning his intelligence, his attitudes, his character. But deeper than all of these external characteristics Paul saw in this person a human being for whom Christ had died. He saw him also as a person whom the Christ was seeking as his disciple. He saw every man as a person who could find the center of his being in living for the Christ who died for him. Paul could look beyond the externals to what a man might become in Christ.

Robert W. Service in a poem entitled "My Madonna" writes:

> I hailed me a woman from the street,
>     Shameless, but, oh, so fair!
> I bade her sit in the model's seat
>     And I painted her sitting there.
>
> I hid all trace of her heart unclean;
>     I painted a babe at her breast;
> I painted her as she might have been
>     If the Worst had been the Best.[26]

Service goes on to describe the connoisseur as he comes and looks at the picture and says, "'Tis Mary, the Mother of God."

The artist was able to see what a person might have been if the worst had been the best. But Paul was able to look at a person and visualize what that person might become if he ceased to live for himself and began to live for the Christ who for his sake died and rose again. Paul had actually seen this kind of transformation take place in the lives of people.

In 1 Corinthians 6:9-11, he lays down the basic principle that the unrighteous will not inherit the kingdom of God. Then he reminds the Corinthians that before their conversion some of them were immoral and others were idolaters. He knows that there are among them those who have been thieves or drunkards or robbers. We must admit that Paul had built a church at Corinth out of people who must have seemed rather unpromising material for the gathering together of a people of God. But after Paul has described the background of some of the members of this church he writes: "But you were washed, you were sanctified, you were justified in the name of the Lord Jesus Christ and in the Spirit of our God." Paul had no illusions as to what people were, but he knew also what they could become in Christ Jesus.

After Paul has made his statement, "We . . . know no man after the flesh," he makes what seems at first a strange detour. He writes: "even though we have known Christ after the flesh, yet now we know him so no more" (A.S.V.). What did Paul mean when he said that even though he had once known Christ after the flesh, he now knew him so no more? And what is the bearing of this statement on his statement that he knows no man after the flesh? We can be reasonably certain that Paul did not have any actual contact with Jesus in the days of his flesh. Peter and John lived with Jesus in the days of his ministry. They could speak as eyewitnesses of the things he said and did. Paul did not have this experience. Paul as the persecutor of the church knew the understanding of Jesus which prevailed among those who had rejected his claim to be the Christ. In his speech to Herod Agrippa, Paul says, "I myself was convinced that I ought to do many things in opposing the name of Jesus of Nazareth" (Acts 26:9). He must at this time have gained a certain factual knowledge of the life of Jesus of Nazareth. Paul the persecutor probably shared with other leaders of the Jews the prevailing conception of the Messiah. He probably looked for a world-conquering Messiah who would break the power of Roman rule and establish the Jews as a ruling people. It may be that he is referring to this conception of the work of the Messiah when he says that he has known Christ after the flesh. It was probably because Jesus of Nazareth as the suffering servant, rejected and crucified, did not fit into this pattern that Paul in the beginning could not accept him as the Messiah. When Paul through his conversion experience became certain that Jesus of Nazareth was the Christ, he had to reject the conception of the Christ that he had once held. The knowledge of the facts concerning the life of Jesus in the days of his flesh made it impossible for Paul to continue to hold to the carnal conception of the Christ.

We must not think that the knowledge of the facts concerning the life of Jesus in the days of his flesh is unimportant. The church's memory of the life of her Lord is preserved for us in the four Gospels. These writings are an absolutely essential part of the New Testament record. The followers of Jesus need to know the facts concerning the things he did and the things he said. We must know the story of Jesus if we are to see "the light of the knowledge of the glory of God in the face of Christ" (2 Corinthians 4:6). Without this knowledge the statement of Jesus, "He who has seen me has seen the Father" (John 14:9), would be without positive content.

But if we are to know the full significance of the story of Jesus in the days of his flesh, we must know more than this story. We must know the Christ who is not "after the flesh" if we are to know the deepest meaning of the record of the words and deeds of Jesus of Nazareth. We must see this event in the perspective of the prologue of John's Gospel in which the Word who was with God becomes flesh and dwells among us. We must know the story of the resurrection in which the Christ returns to manifest himself to his disciples as being alive. We must understand what the first Christians meant when they spoke of his ascension to the Father and of his sitting at the right hand of God. We must enter with them into their consciousness of his spiritual presence with his people. We must understand them as they looked for the Savior from heaven to bring to an end the present world order. We must believe in the living Lord who is forever with his people if we are to know the Christ who is the Savior of the world today. We must continually return to the story of Jesus in the days of his flesh, but this story must always be seen in the light of the whole New Testament testimony as to who HE is.

It is the knowledge of the Christ who is not "after the flesh" that makes it impossible for Paul to know any man after the flesh. And it is the knowledge of this Christ as present in his church today that makes it impossible for Christians to be content to know men after the flesh. We must see every human being as a person who has an immortal soul. We must know that the living Christ loves this person and that it is his will for this person to come to know him and to live for him. He has the power to turn this person from a life of selfishness and sin to a life of loving obedience to him. It is in this setting that Paul says that if anyone is in Christ, he is a new creation. The Christ has the power to forgive our sins and to make of us a new creation. He has the power to give to those who receive him the capacity to become sons of God. If any man be in Christ, "the old has passed away, behold, the new has come" (2 Corinthians 5:17).

In the routine of his dealing with people, however, Paul had to make his judgments according to the flesh. He tells Timothy that Alexander the coppersmith has done him much harm. He warns

Timothy to beware of him (2 Timothy 4:14-15). He is unwilling to take Mark on a second journey after he has failed him on the first. He says that Demas has deserted him because he is in love with this present world (2 Timothy 4:10). He is outspoken in his tributes to Timothy and Titus. Like everyone else, he had to make his judgments of people on the basis of his observation of them. But he never failed to see in every human being an immortal soul, a person capable of an eternal destiny. He knew that the love of Christ went out to every human being. He knew that he was the bearer of the message of the Christ, and his deepest concern was to communicate this message in such a way that men would respond in faith, love, and obedience. Because the church today knows the Christ who is not according to the flesh she must never be content merely to know men according to the flesh. She must see every human being as he is and also as an immortal soul whom the Christ would call to be his follower and to become an heir of eternal life.

# ACKNOWLEDGMENTS

1. Revised Standard Version, 1952 edition. This verse has been translated differently in the edition revised in 1959.

2. Translation as given in Sanday and Headlam, *The Epistle to the Romans,* p. 216, in *The International Critical Commentary.* (New York: Charles Scribner's Sons, 1926.)

3. Anonymous, 1880.

4. Robert Browning, "An Epistle, containing the Strange Medical Experience of Karshish, the Arab Physician," in *The Complete Poetic and Dramatic Works of Robert Browning,* p. 340. (Boston: Houghton Mifflin Company, 1895.)

5. *Ibid.,* pp. 340-341.

6. From "A General Confession," in *The Book of Common Prayer,* p. 23. (Greenwich, Conn.: The Seabury Press, 1952.)

7. Robert Browning, "With Francis Furini," pp. 968-969, from *Parleyings with Certain People of Importance in Their Day* in Browning's Complete Works.

8. Robert Browning, "Bishop Blougram's Apology," p. 355.

9. From "Mandalay," stanza 6, in *Collected Verse of Rudyard Kipling.* (New York: Doubleday, Page and Company, 1917.)

10. *The Westminster Shorter Catechism,* Answer to Question 14.

11. Karl Barth, *Theological Existence To-day!,* p. 52. (London: Hodder and Stoughton, 1933.)

12. Frederic W. H. Myers, *Saint Paul,* p. 34. (London and New York: Macmillan & Co., 1896.)

13. Alfred, Lord Tennyson, "Guinevere," from *Idylls of the King,* in *The Poetic and Dramatic Works of Alfred, Lord Tennyson.* (Boston: Houghton Mifflin Company, 1899.)

14. Sanday and Headlam, *op. cit.,* p. 216.

15. Alfred, Lord Tennyson, *In Memoriam A. H. H.,* section i.

16. Sanday and Headlam, *op. cit.,* p. 216.

17. Anonymous, "Lord, Take Away Pain," in *1000 Quotable Poems,* Volume One, p. 26. (Chicago: Willett, Clark & Company, 1937.)

18. Alfred, Lord Tennyson, "Vastness," stanza ii.

19. Hugh Martin, *The Faith of Robert Browning,* pp. 97-98. (London:

SCM Press, Ltd., 1963; Richmond: John Knox Press, 1964.) The rearrangement of the last lines of "Cleon" is Dr. Martin's.

20. Psalm 103:7-8, 17-18.

21. *The Westminster Shorter Catechism,* Answer to Question 87.

22. Hugh Martin, *op. cit.,* p. 118.

23. K., "How Firm a Foundation," in Rippon's *A Selection of Hymns,* 1787. (No. 369 in *The Hymnbook.*)

24. Quoted by E. T. Thompson in *Through the Ages* (Teacher's Book), p. 37. (Richmond: The CLC Press, 1965.)

25. R. St. John Parry, *The First Epistle of Paul the Apostle to the Corinthians,* p. 174. (Cambridge: Cambridge University Press, 1916.)

26. Robert W. Service, "My Madonna," in *The Spell of the Yukon and Other Verses.* (New York: Dodd, Mead & Company, 1907.) Used by permission of the publishers.

**Dat**